ORDINARY GLORY

Finding Grace in the Commonplace

Dane Fowlkes

ISBN 978-1-63575-005-8 (Paperback)
ISBN 978-1-63575-006-5 (Digital)

ORDINARY GLORY: Finding Grace in the Commonplace. All rights reserved. No part of this book may be used or reproduced in any manner whatsoever without written permission except in the case of brief quotations embodied in critical articles and reviews.

FIRST EDITION

Copyright © 2017 by Dane Fowlkes
All rights reserved. No part of this publication may be reproduced, distributed, or transmitted in any form or by any means, including photocopying, recording, or other electronic or mechanical methods without the prior written permission of the publisher. For permission requests, solicit the publisher via the address below.

Christian Faith Publishing, Inc.
296 Chestnut Street
Meadville, PA 16335
www.christianfaithpublishing.com

Printed in the United States of America

Dedication

To my loving wife, Jo Beth,
in whose eyes I find God's grace every morning;

and to my grandchildren,
I can only hope that something I leave behind from
my journey will assist you on your own

FOREWORD

Ordinary. Commonplace. Prior to reading *Ordinary Glory: Finding Grace in the Commonplace* by Dane Fowlkes, I would have had difficulty imagining how those words could have been used in any manner in a discussion or book relating to God's grace. Granted, it was readily apparent that the author's intent was not to use these words to describe that grace, but I was intrigued by how a gift as powerful and wonderful as God's love, mercy, and kindness could be found in ordinary, commonplace settings and experiences. My personal perception of his grace had become somewhat skewed in that examples of grace in my life were always obvious and clearly divine gifts that were overwhelmingly remarkable and significant. The continued love and devotion of my wife, the birth of my children and grandchildren, resolution of serious health issues, safe deliverance from extreme danger and violence are but some of the examples of God's grace realized in my own experience. The concept that God's love, kindness, and goodness were not one-time gifts but continue to be showered upon me every living moment were overshadowed by more obvious manifestations as the examples mentioned above. The not-so-obvious gifts are in no way any less spectacular or important, simply more difficult to detect. This is especially so when they are taken for granted over an extended period of time.

When it comes to recognizing, appreciating, and savoring the beauty of God's creation, my vision has always been twenty-twenty. It doesn't have to be a phenomenally colorful sunset, a beautiful rose in bloom, a newborn's smile, or the morning serenade of mockingbirds to fill me with praise and gratitude to our Creator. Puffy white cumulus clouds floating across an azure sky, the symmetry of a spider's web glistening with morning dew in sunlight, or the intricate veins of a cottonwood leaf all possess a visual beauty rivaling that of the most fantastic mountain range or summer sunset for those capable of seeing and recognizing God's less conspicuous handiwork. In *Ordinary Glory*, Dr. Fowlkes shares observations and experiences that demonstrate God's grace in a number of everyday situations and conditions that we have all likely experienced. Like detecting beauty in unlikely places such as a leaf or spider web, he provides examples of grace found in areas where we may not have previously recognized its presence—in familiar relationships and seemingly mundane interactions with family, friends, and even strangers. The real trick, at least for me, is discerning it for what it is. Jesus repeats throughout Scripture that those with eyes should see and those with ears should hear. More than once while reading *Ordinary Glory*, I felt the need to be fitted with glasses. Dane does a masterful job of pointing out situations where I, too, had experienced yet had not recognized, much less appreciated the presence of grace. Repeatedly, his observations made me think, *Yes, I know exactly what he's talking about....never thought of it that way, but he's right. God's handprint is all over that.*

Dr. Fowlkes provides a perspective and clear writing style I find refreshing and enjoyable to read. In *Ordinary Glory*, the author does not delve into deep theological theory, debate, history, or the extraneous issues related thereto. He takes common situations most all of us have experienced or endured and provides easily understandable explanation of how God is present in our lives, showering us with His love even though we've done nothing to deserve it. From my point of view, the beauty and value of *Ordinary Glory* is that it encourages a sense of enlightenment that sharpens my vision and, more importantly, refines my discernment capabilities to better recognize God's grace in my own life in situations and ways I previously would not have believed possible. I now enjoy a depth of clarity that was not previously present; God's grace is now almost as clearly visible to me as the beauty of his creation. This is no ordinary or commonplace achievement. Dane has done an exceptional job, and it is my wish that you find *Ordinary Glory* as enjoyable, enlightening, and valuable as have I.

Kirby W. Dendy
Chief of the Texas Rangers (Retired)

CONTENTS

Acknowledgments 9
Preface...11
Introduction..13
1. Wounds...19
2. Influence..31
3. Ourselves..45
4. Community...63
5. Worship..81
6. Surrender...93
7. Family 109
8. Transitions..131
Epilogue..151

ACKNOWLEDGMENTS

Writing may be a labor of love, but as such is rarely a solitary effort. I doubt seriously that I ever have or ever will own an original thought; my thinking and, as a result, my writing is the natural consequence and confluence of many streams, all of which bear names and familiar faces. I am indebted to each that has poured knowingly or unwittingly into this common life. Having admitted as much, I must herald certain ones for their intentional influence.

Grandma Richey, as she was affectionately known, quietly taught by example; Irish frugality forged through the Great Depression did not prevent love from flourishing in her humble white-frame house. My parents not only chose me as their adopted son, but invested everything a child could ask for, if indeed a child could know enough to ask. Kirby took time from grandchildren and ranch building to lend a careful eye and well-crafted foreword. Roddy critiqued with an editor's eye, which in turn provided a literary frame with which to work. Jo Beth, who inspires every day through strength of character and transparent beauty, has encouraged my writing from the outset of our love story. A gifted communicator in her own right, her first gift after agreeing to marry me was a book entitled *Lines on the Water* in which she inscribed

> *To Dane—*
> *I love you with "A River Kind of Love." I hope this book is more inspiration to you in your own writing.*
> *Jo*

Finally, I owe an insurmountable debt to my grandchildren, who teach me more about grace than I have learned in any classroom or from any book.

PREFACE

My wife asked two reasonable questions at the outset of this project: "Why are you writing?" and "Who do you expect to read what you've written?" The first was easy to answer because I initially set out to write something for my grandchildren. I decided that I wanted a way of leaving something behind that would say I was here and that would tell what I had wanted to say to them in person but lacked either opportunity or courage. Although closely related to the first, the second question deserves more explanation. Having stated that I write as *Papa* (the term my grandchildren use when addressing me), I must admit that there is more to my motivation. I've had in mind for some time to encourage average believers and inspire run-of-the mill skeptics; the problem with that is that there are, after all, no *average* believers or *run-of-the-mill* skeptics. We are, each of us, extraordinary individuals stumbling through, scaling over, or staggering under the ordinary.

"It is what it is." I caught myself saying so the other day without thinking about my meaning or its wider implication. Quite honestly, I uttered it in a less-than-positive vein. Burdened by limitations within myself, frustration surfaced as a cliché, but, as is the case with most clichés, the trite and hackneyed expression was grounded in truth. Life is what it is, which makes it all the more critical that we see ourselves as we are—extraordinary harbingers of the divine, and every moment as it is—colored beautifully by grace. The practice of discerning grace in unexpected ways during the very non-surprising routines of life continues to dominate my thinking and captivate my imagination. Life changes suddenly for some, but for most of us, transformation comes slowly, imperceptibly. Alterations in patterns of living and the people experiencing them often go unnoticed until something causes us to pause and reflect. We can learn a lot about ourselves and our Maker if we know where to look.

My prayer is that what you are about to read will lead you to pause and reflect. If you choose along the way to set the book aside and thoughtfully stare into space, or, more importantly, into yourself, I will have fulfilled my purpose in writing. I have chosen certain experiences that I believe illustrate the weight of glory in ordinary human experience, and have grouped them according to broad themes with which you will likely be able to identify. Through the stories that follow, I hope to say something meaningful to extraordinary people about the grace that transforms what is admittedly common into what is inexplicably uncommon. My prayer for every reader is the same as it is for my grandchildren—that you will discover in these pages a comfortable companion for the journey, or a memory you didn't know was yours that you share with others. May you better detect the glory in the ordinary and be encouraged to find grace in the commonplace.

Bosqueville 2016

INTRODUCTION

One life on this earth is all that we get, whether it is enough or not enough, and the obvious conclusion would seem to be that at the very least we are fools if we do not live it as fully and bravely and beautifully as we can.
—Frederick Buechner

The answer must be I think that beauty and grace are performed whether or not we will or sense them. The least we can do is try to be there.
—Annie Dillard

I write from personal experience that heaven is living in close proximity to whom and what one loves most. In that respect, I have found paradise; more accurately, paradise has found me. The most discerning, scintillating, and alluring woman I've ever known calls me *darling*; precocious yet precious grandchildren, daughters, and sons-in-law call me *Papa*, and intriguing neighbors call me *friend*. I am blessed with residential space to breathe apart from urban interference; plank fencing marks our boundaries rather than cement sidewalks, and caliche replaces asphalt. Prominent sounds in our distance are not those of urban sprawl; instead, barred owls beckon to one another with sounds we call monkey chatter, kingfishers rattle back and forth over the surface of the pond, and an ever-present phoebe wheezes on a nearby limb. Red oaks on the sunrise side of our house are losing their struggle against a stiff north wind, the elms having given up the fight a few weeks ago. Kimberly queens are nestled warmly in the greenhouse next to foxtail and bird's-nest ferns, grapevines, and roses, glad for the refuge from freezing temperatures. Tree fatigue is everywhere; leaves fall like amber, orange, and purple snow. My least favorite tree makes the biggest soiree of all, and to this day, I cannot imagine why the Creator dreamed up sweet gums, replete with prickly balls that somehow always find their way beneath my feet; fall foliage is its one almost-redeeming attribute.

There is something oddly warming about this chilly transition. Leaves shrivel from the cold but do not call attention to the dying. Autumn brushes them beautiful before winter robs of pigment, leaving me with hope for the same before my own demise. The time is too fast approaching when color will fade in more than my hair and I too become brittle and broken; until then, allow me the splendor of *this* moment. Permit me the realization of wishes, the scratching off of bucket lists, the jubilance of self-expression, the consolation of completion. Color my own transition to winter beautiful, not for the sake of attracting admirers but for God's renown. Dylan Thomas misunderstood seasons: *do* go gentle into that good night, and *do not* rage against the dying of the light. Grace unfolds through the natural rhythms of life, persisting riverlike over tranquil pools as well as stony shoals. Ours is to reflect to the end the grace that makes each moment a beginning.

"Listening while living" is an art form worth learning. Life seems at times like a succession of converging and divergent tragedies, at once interconnected and then again, disparate. Unfortunately, our earthbound perspective is linear and we strain to see ahead and behind without the ability to focus properly on either. We do not realize that this "right now" perspective is actually a grace-gift. Jesus expresses it eloquently:

> *Therefore, do not be anxious about tomorrow, for tomorrow will be anxious for itself. Sufficient for the day is its own trouble.*[1]

---

[1] Matthew 6:34 (ESV)

In other words, we have right now, not yesterday or tomorrow. Surrender *this* moment. Celebrate *this* day. Create *this* memory. Love immediately and passionately. Do what lies at hand, and you just may find the dividend is eternal.

About the time I retreat within my struggle as to whether or not there is rhyme or reason to my current demands and immediate pressures, I'm rescued by a visit from grandchildren. Such was the case when two-year-old Hannah Beth spent the evening with us while big sister went to the county fair. My assignment upon arriving home from a business trip was to distract Hannah, thereby allowing my wife to complete an embroidery project with a friend. Hannah and I took to the great out-of-doors hand in hand, and I watched with fascination as she reached down to examine every fallen leaf, place it in my hands, wait for me to "ooh and aah," then retrieve and gently return it to its previous spot on the grass. Hannah knows how to enjoy the moment, undisturbed by the past and unencumbered by anything future. In short order, my precious companion reminded me of the weightiest theology I've ever learned: "All moments are key moments, and life itself is grace."[2] The clearest signal of transcendence is that *this* moment, in and of itself, matters enormously. Eternity begins right now.

My wife heard and spotted them first. She always does. We were on the return portion of our customary evening walk atop Lake Waco dam, facing into a north breeze that made me anticipate upcoming brisk winter walks that will be, quite literally, breathtaking. Since my hearing has never been quite up to snuff, subtle nuances of sound often escape me, which explains why she paused and looked up toward the westerly thunderheads while I maintained rhythm of pumping arms and straining footfall. When she vanished from my periphery, I slowed and turned, and then followed her gaze skyward.

"Do you hear them?" she asked.

"Hear who?" I replied.

"The geese."

---

[2] Frederick Buechner, *Now and Then: A Memoir of Vocation* (New York: HarperOne, 1991).

We aren't tree huggers in a political sense, but my wife and I definitely appreciate and are drawn to the natural side of living. We own more bird feeders than pretty much anything else, and erected a deer feeder several years ago in the pasture behind our home—not to lure deer to their death, but to keep them well fed in winter. As a result, simple events that fly below the radar for most, like hummingbirds disappearing for warmer environs and the honking of geese high above or near the horizon, command our attention. When I finally heard what had stopped my wife in her tracks, I strained to find visual evidence of audible clues, and detected the pulsating ribbon of geese snaking its way above black- and blue-mottled clouds toward the southern horizon. It was in that moment that my wife gripped my arm and jerked me to attention. Starboard of the skein of geese, a bald eagle came into focus almost directly overhead. We have enjoyed rare sightings of eagles on the periphery of Lake Waco before, so we had no problem identifying the proud raptor. I attempted to capture the image with my iPhone, but vision was rendered useless by the blinding sun. Had it not been for the geese, we would not have seen the eagle.

Geese brandish their own strain of beauty, but they aren't exactly exotic creatures. In fact, we have friends living on Lake Athens that loathe them because of their propensity to blanket a lawn with poop. Prewinter geese sorties are pleasant to behold, but never catch one by surprise. They are somewhat expected, even taken for granted, until seen winging it next to eagles. Thank God for the ordinary events and individuals that bring the larger picture into focus. I better detect what God is up to when I see him in juxtaposition to my grandchildren, the cashier that annoys me, the colleague with cancer, the relative that talks nonstop out of loneliness, the friend agonizing over a prodigal child, a church that has lost its way. The ordinary yields glimpses of glory when I pay attention.

I am praying differently these days, not so much to know God's will any longer but, instead, simply to recognize him in the commonplace. This moment perches precariously on a knife-edge, animation suspended between memory and mystery. Lean too far behind and tumble into remorse, regret, reprise, repeat. Stretch too intensely toward tomorrow and drift into fog, fantasy, make-believe. Either behind or ahead is dysfunction. To live *this* breath in healthy tension with present attention, that is the divine mandate—nothing less than relentless intersection, perpetual incarnation. Created in the image of "I am", "*we are*" abiding best in our Heavenly Father when we extol his grace that benefits this breath and embrace the exhilaration of not living in the wake of what we once were. Every day matters; our daily challenge is to recognize what matters most. To be completely honest, that has changed for me over the years. I've often wrestled with the inclination to lose sight of the value of this instant while straining to predict the next and strategize accordingly, but I am learning that what happened or did not occur yesterday pales in significance with what I do right now; life does count, and this very moment matters enormously. Mercy is at hand in abundance when I allow myself to detect the weight of glory in the mundane and ordinary. Grace is now and grace is here; grace is always present tense.

ONE

Wounds

> *Pay attention to the things that bring a tear to your eye or a lump in your throat because they are signs that the holy is drawing near.*
> —Frederick Buechner

I like a party as much as the next guy, but confess that I wasn't able to generate much enthusiasm for our staff Christmas party. No reflection on my colleagues or an indictment on me, but everything about it seemed out of sync for some reason. Perhaps I felt that way because my wife couldn't come, or it may have been the seventy-degree temperatures with high humidity, which only felt like Christmas in that it reminded me of childhood Decembers on the Gulf Coast in Port Arthur. Regardless, I sat outside among several couples, alone with my thoughts, paper plate full of lasagna and french bread balanced on my legs, a cup of coffee at hand, situated near a propane heater that quietly effused warmth to the outdoor deck.

In an effort to be polite, I addressed the young man seated across from me. Intending to engage in nothing more than small talk, I asked casually about his work and family. His response arrested me from my party funk, and I sat spellbound for the next fifteen minutes as he narrated how life had changed for him since he and his wife almost lost their two-year-old son when he fell into a rural pond last year. His voice broke slightly as he ended the story by saying that the whole experience was a wound that held him nearer to the heart of God, and that he never wanted it to completely heal. He had tears in his eyes. I had a lump in my throat. We sat in silence; a simple candlelit patio transformed into sacred space by the reminder that we will never be like Christ without a wound.

†

It is easy to be dogmatic until the dog barks at *you*. Sunday morning began much the same as any other: two cups of coffee, a blueberry bagel slathered with lite cream cheese (to appease my diet-conscious wife), numerous read-throughs of the morning's soon-to-be-delivered sermon, and intermittent prayer. Like clockwork, we traveled down Rock Creek Road to a little white-frame church where nothing memorable happened during the worship service that followed, including my preaching. We returned home as we do most Sundays after church; I changed into jeans and an old college sweatshirt and set about to do nothing in particular—one of the reasons I love Sunday afternoons. During the interlude leading up to lunch, I received a text message from my high school senior daughter. Text messages are common occurrences these days and notoriously void of emotion, but this one conjured up plenty on my part: "Dad, I need to talk to you. Please call when you can." Without knowing what she meant, I did what she asked and placed the call. She answered, and I asked what was on her mind. She said, "Dad, I don't want to tell you. Can't you just guess and I'll let you know when you get it right?" All I could think to say was what I honestly believe: "No matter what you have to tell me, nothing will change the fact that you're my daughter and I will always love you." Interminable silence followed, broken finally by what I somehow already knew: "I'm pregnant." Two simple words, yet profound enough to change the world.

I appreciate anyone's honest struggle with what to do with those two words, but must confess a vested interest in every human outcome of the debate. Born to an unwed mother in 1960, I would have had a damning designation on my birth certificate were it not for the tireless efforts of Edna Gladney on behalf of children like me some twenty years previous. As bad as it would have been to have a prejudiced label on my birth certificate, the good news is that I have a birth certificate. The even better news is that my birth mother had the courage to enter Sellers

Baptist Home in New Orleans and gift me to Henry and Lois, a couple with hearts large enough to allow a child to flourish in the arms of great nourishing love. I would never denigrate that poor young woman's angst over yielding her child, and, in fact, attempt consciously to live in such a way as to validate the outcome of her decision. Two things get lost in the debate over choice versus life: the enduring turmoil of the mother-in-waiting, and the enduring destiny of the child-in-waiting.

For those who uphold the individual's choice as superior to the unborn child, you will, no doubt, abhor my opposition to your position. For those who vilify the individual in support of a moral dilemma, you must excuse my sensitivity to the turmoil of the woman. I have been and continue to be profoundly altered by the courage of my daughter who followed the first two words with four others: "I'm having this baby." The bottom line is this: I write not on this critical issue as physician, scientist, theologian—liberal or conservative; I speak as a survivor, and write as a father.

He stopped by our home in order to share some of his struggles; he needed a pastor, and I was the one most geographically accessible. What he told was one part confession, another part philosophy, and a final part conjecture; he closed with a declaration of septic pessimism, "I can see the handwriting on the wall." Grief and regret are siblings, if not identical twins; they combined to make it impossible for my acquaintance to see the forest of God's mercy for the trees of his own making. The man's dilemma reminded me of two related but radically different biblical concepts with which I identify most naturally and fully. The first is that we are all fatally flawed creatures. The second is that the only thing that distinguishes the believer from the unbeliever is that she or he recognizes and embraces God's grace as the only remedy for her or his flaws. Without even trying, I am a walking, talking, daily illustration of the first truth. If you watch closely or listen to me long enough, you will readily observe my flawed character. Over time, I will exhibit the negative attributes of every biblical character read about with horror or disdain; given enough rope to hang myself, I take the fall every time. In fact, there seems to be no bottom to the depths to which I can and do fall, no limit to the disappointment I evoke in those who know and expect more from me. More profoundly, I am adept at disappointing myself.

Fortunately, the second truth is made even more obvious when observing God's grace in relief. I've overheard myself at times thinking, *Apart from the grace of God, there go I*, when the truth is that I am every bit as guilt-riddled as every guilty person who has or ever will live. Scripture shouts my story when it declares, "There is nothing good in me"[3] and "My righteousness is as filthy rags in the sight of God,"[4] but in the same breath, it sings my song, "Amazing grace, how sweet the sound, that saved a wretch like me." My struggle is not in finding God's pardon, it is in accepting God's forgiveness and moving on. Guilt binds my heart and gags my mouth, but grace explodes the chains. The man on our front porch was correct—there is handwriting on the wall. If we know where to look, we will detect in divine script what Brennan Manning calls the "signature of Jesus." Grace transforms flawed human beings into trophies of God's power and love.

I could swap stories of regret until the cows come home, but what good would that do? Unless you were born today, each of us has a past to move beyond; sadly, some of us work our way back to the pain all too often. If not careful, I return routinely to be scorched by my past, self-inflicting the hurt of remembering, like my memory of the man who died hating me.

We were friends, spending more than a few hours together in his johnboat fishing for largemouth in the stump heavy waters of Toledo Bend; beyond that, I was his pastor. Everything changed when a certain church dispute left me standing on principle but losing a friend. I wouldn't budge, and Encil couldn't forgive, so he simply left. He would drive his wife to church in a faded green Dodge pickup, drop her off to

---

[3] Romans 7:18 (KJV).
[4] Isaiah 64:6 (KJV).

sing in the choir, and return to collect Mozelle each Sunday when the service ended. Eventually I moved on as young pastors are wont to do and lost track of them, but Encil apparently never forgot me. A couple of years later, I learned that he had been hospitalized for a terminal condition, and I decided to go and see him—perhaps we could bury the hatchet, or at least dull its edge. The visit is imprinted on my memory like a sepia negative. I entered the room and saw Encil lying in bed, facing forward toward a small elevated television screen. His wife was seated between the bed and door, and upon recognizing me, she stood and approached. As I began to speak softly to her, he turned in bed and faced the wall away from me. Mozelle said flatly that she thought it best for me to leave. I did, and learned a short time later that he had passed. Encil died hating me, and I've spent the past thirty years contemplating how I would rewrite the ending if I could.

There's a reason for remembering; memory is as much about today as it is yesterday. "'It's a poor sort of memory that only works backwards,' says the White Queen to Alice."[5] God created memory so that I may learn from my past for the purpose of either repeating or avoiding it. "Scars have the strange power to remind us that our past is real."[6] However, regret is the enemy of peace. Arthur Miller writes, "Maybe all one can do is hope to end up with the right regrets," but he is wrong.[7] Regret may be inevitable, yet it need not be the last word; healing is available to every intrepid heart. Courage is required to own up to one's past and take responsibility for it, but it takes as much spiritual fortitude to embrace God's forgiveness and extend the same to others. Expressing gratitude for God and every other person you can think of is no mere psychological ploy; genuine thankfulness is not tricking me or God into granting peace. Gratitude today heals my hurt from yesterday and qualifies me for joy tomorrow. Thanksgiving is the shortest road to recovery.

---

[5] Lewis Carroll, *Alice's Adventures in Wonderland and through the Looking Glass* (New York: Bantam Classics, 1984).

[6] Cormac McCarthy, *All the Pretty Horses* (New York: Pan MacMillan, 2012).

[7] Arthur Miller, *The Ride Down Mt. Morgan* (New York: Penguin Books, 1991).

Try as I might, I cannot reason with grief. All evidence indicated that my father-in-law was losing his struggle with Alzheimer's. He had been declining for more than two years, so logic declared that this would be for the better. Reason chimed in that Popi had already left us some time before, and theology insisted he would soon be in a better place. I cannot and would not argue against logic, reason, or theology; the fact of the matter is, I agree. Alzheimer's is an insidious mystery, and release from its ghastly grip is nothing, if not an improvement. Having admitted all associated truth, it hurts to lose a family member we love. It pierces to know we will never see him again in this life. Grief is a wound that resists healing; a loss that is impossible to endure without connecting it to previous, seemingly unrelated, losses. When my mother died, I instantly grieved my father's passing fifteen years earlier. As we faced my father-in-law's pending departure, I grieved the loss of my own mother. There is nothing logical about such a practice of association. Perhaps this connecting of darkened dots eases back the corner slightly on the mystery of life—we were created for relationship and cannot understand life in isolation. Each is a part of another, even without an associated genealogy.

The world is small in a dying person's room. All concerns shrink to the immediate context, and waiting turns to remembering out loud in mostly whispered tones, as if sitting in a childhood library. I confess that I was secretly selfish in the interlude. As I witnessed the tangible compassion of family and the nearness of love, I gained inexplicable comfort in anticipating the same at my own curtain call. There may be nothing nearer to the heart of God than this, to love and be loved in return. Buechner wrote about *A Room Called Remember*, but I sat in a room called peace. There is a giftedness about watching life draw to a gradual close without strain or struggle—silent, peaceful. Popi's breathing slowed and would soon stop altogether, and according to every indication, it would go momentarily unnoticed when it happened. In a whitewashed room such as this, life scales back to the essentials—a breath, a heartbeat, a swallowing. And suddenly, what matters most in all the world is this sacred sharing of each slowing breath. In the stillness, I heard my heart whisper,

"Cherish better each moment with the ones you love. Savor more sweetly your own daily gifts."

> *We prevent God from giving us the great spiritual gifts He has in store for us, because we do not give thanks for daily gifts . . . Only he who gives thanks for little things receives the big things.*[8]

Fortunately, mourning may be superimposed on watermarks of joy. Such is the normal human response to a loved one's release from Alzheimer's ravaged effects. I do not hesitate to admit that I miss Popi and dread the pang of all future family gatherings without him. My *boccie* adversary was taken from me, but I could not succumb to the hurt of absence without remembering the last time we played and how I had to remind him each turn of the rules of the game he previously knew so well. Looking down upon his shrinking frame, I did not want him to go, yet silently prayed he would. And now he has, and I appeal to heaven that the peace that is now Popi's will soften the ragged corners of grief for those of us who remain. I am not intelligent enough to explain in metaphysical detail what takes place when breath and heartbeat cease, but I am wise enough to admit that I do not know how to explain it. Some say death is the start of a gradual journey toward the ultimate reunion. My thoughts run counter to such linear speculation, for I see heaven as a matter of dimension, not distance. Heaven is not a far-off place—some biblical Land of Oz—and the Father is not, as Bette Midler sang, "in the distance." Scripture throbs with passionate cadence that God is near, making heaven not a trip, but merely a step—what Marcus Borg calls "Meeting Jesus Again for the First Time."[9] For all I'm worth, I believe that Popi has now met Jesus again for the first time; the only waiting for him is for the opportunity to introduce us.

---

[8] Dietrich Bonhoeffer, *Life Together: The Classic Exploration of Faith in Christian Community* (New York: HarperOne, 2009).

[9] Marcus Borg, *Meeting Jesus Again for the First Time* (New York: HarperOne, 1995).

DANE FOWLKES

We worship God through our questions.
—Abraham Joshua Heschel

I enjoy waking early, but rarely do much more with the stillness than accompany morning coffee with meditation. These are not moments for *doing* so much as *being;* reflection fuels response. One particular winter morning not long after Popi was released from his confused confines of clay, I shoved aside the sermon that insisted on intruding and allowed myself to settle on daydreaming about heaven. It feels somehow natural to think about death while peering through glazed windows at weighted skies and naked trees. A gray and barren horizon makes it suddenly a strain to remember warmth and light and hope, as recent as the day before. What complicates such mornings for me is that considering the endlessness of days creates honest inner turmoil hastened by a barbed question—will life end with death? Years ago, as a young pastor, I meticulously recorded funerals officiated in a massive blank-lined volume bound for such a purpose (perhaps thinking that by writing names in a book, I might grant them immortality), but I have long since abandoned the practice. I have lost count of how many times I have stood behind podiums or beside coffins pronouncing hope that we are presiding not over an end, but an endless beginning. Reciting dog-eared scriptures for the comfort of those lagging behind in the run to see Jesus, I sincerely deliver discourses on the eternal, but always with a twinge of wonder. Can such platinum hope prove true? Will I one day blink in death only to find myself transfigured? Is it possible that my own gray horizon might yield to light grander than anything I've read about or imagined? Do not consider me a skeptic; instead, number me among those who cannot honestly declare we have no questions, but journey with confidence that we are embraced by the Answer.

ORDINARY GLORY

Truth walks toward us on the paths of our questions. As soon as you think you have the answer, you have closed the path and may miss vital new information. Wait awhile in the stillness, and do not rush to conclusion no matter how uncomfortable the unknowing.
—Jaqueline Winspear[10]

We sat across from one another, with not much in common except a question. I wasn't exactly sure how he had found me, but here we were, sipping coffee, exchanging pleasantries, edging closer to the reason we had agreed to meet in the first place. I asked what I could do for him and heard him say that he was spiritually dry as toast and looking for someone to help him revive what was left of his Christian experience. The crux of the matter was that he was more disillusioned with himself than with God, with the Almighty running a close second. Years of Christian ministry had obscured the reason for that service, leaving him in a downward spiral of guilt and dissatisfaction. When I asked the bottom line of his apparent misery, he replied, "I'm not sure if any of this is real, and I don't see how I can play the game any longer. I have more questions than I do answers." The silence was tangible between us. His downward stare reflected a defeated heart, but he raised eyebrows and his gaze when I finally said, "We honor God most by the questions we ask. It's when we begin to question that we draw closest to the heart of God."

God speaks more clearly to us through questions than is possible when we're convinced we have all the answers. When we query, our mind remains open; when we focus on answers, it is clear that our minds are made up, which is actually a curious phrase. Saying I have my mind made up sounds on par with making my bed or having poached eggs for breakfast. Faith is not that neat, simple, or bland; and questions are not the enemy of faith—arrogance is. Questioning is not doubting because it anticipates an answer, making it great faith and even greater hope. An unlikely source of inspiration at this point is Saint Thomas. "Doubting

---

10   Jaqueline Winspear, *Maisie Dobbs* (New York: Penguin, 2003), 32.

Thomas," as he is more commonly known, has received a bad rap over the past two thousand years, likely because his honesty hits a little too close to home. The apostolic doubter dared say what he was thinking, and church history has been uncomfortable with him ever since. I appreciate Didymus much more these days, and not just because tradition says he went on to spread the Gospel throughout India, dying in the process. I am wary of those who claim to have cornered the market when it comes to knowing God and who peddle their trademark spirituality accordingly. I am uncomfortable when someone speaks with *cocksuredness* about what Scripture calls mystery, and when anyone attempts to pigeonhole another's faith narrative according to their own. The moment I am able to fully explain God, he ceases to be, which explains my affinity for those who write in shadows of divine mystery and allow room for trial and error, as well as honest exploration. I received a letter not long ago from a friend responding to my request for constructive criticism on my writing, and his comments stopped me in my tracks:

> *One of my criticisms of virtually every sermonizer I have ever heard is their unwillingness and/or inability to sensibly ponder the basic questions and mysteries of life, death and the hereafter and their clear inadequacies to use Scripture, denominational dogma and ministerial learning to deal honestly with those questions and mysteries. . . . The intellectual dishonesty of ministers is, at times, breathtaking.*

His final statement is the one that stuns—"intellectual dishonesty of ministers." Call it eloquent dissatisfaction if you like, the fulcrum of Thomas's uneasiness was that he was seeking after the real Jesus and would accept no imitations. If there is anything at all to embrace in religion, it is intellectual and spiritual honesty. One biographer describes Frederick Buechner's conversion in compatible terms:

> *It was the culmination of a secret seeking in his life and the embarkation upon a further phase of his*

journey, now shaped by a Christian faith that had about it a delicate, indelible ambiguity.[11]

I love that phrase, "indelible ambiguity," and want it to be true of my own journey—unapologetically seeking space to ponder, fusing faith with "gratitude for having received a great gift."[12] Convinced that Christ is the answer, we are free to invest a lifetime learning from questions that matter most.

☨

> *I know what torment this is, but I can only see it (doubt), in myself anyway, as the process by which faith is deepened. A faith that just accepts is a child's faith and all right for children, but eventually you have to grow religiously as every other way, though some never do. What people don't realize is how much religion costs. They think faith is a big electric blanket, when of course it is the cross. It is much harder to believe than not to believe. If you feel you can't believe, you must at least do this: keep an open mind. Keep it open toward faith, keep wanting it, keep asking for it, and leave the rest to God.*
> —Flannery O'Connor[13]

Decisions define, and, at times, redefine us. I learned this at my lowest juncture from an unlikely source. For as long as I can remember, my only ambition has been to serve the Lord Jesus Christ as my life's

---

[11] Marjorie Casebier McCoy, *Frederick Buechner: Novelist and Theologian of the Lost and Found* (San Francisco: Harper & Row, Publishers, 1988).

[12] Ibid.

[13] Flannery O'Connor, *The Habit of Being: Letters of Flannery O'Connor* (New York: Farrar, Strauss and Giroux, 1988).

calling. That passion carried me into several pastorates, propelled me through nearly a decade of missionary service, and, ultimately, fueled a great deal of internal conflict when faced with a decision that threatened to strip it all away. The shoe dropped when I determined that the future well-being of my children carried more weight than preserving my vocation; Christians are adept at discarding divorced ministers with little regard for the truth. I crossed the line of demarcation for all the right reasons, but lines crossed leave scars that resist healing. "Scars tell stories. Scars mean survival. Scars mean you showed up for the fight rather than running from it." What Genevieve Smythe writes may be true, but scars are not calluses; they commonly mark the spot of internal damage that stubbornly refuses to heal, like the greater threat lurking underneath an iridescent iceberg.

Fortunately for me, grace brushed across my life when I was most vulnerable, the point at which shame threatened to lead down innumerable deadly trails. Grace always has a face, and the one I encountered in my despair was an unshaven aging prison psychologist. He and his wife were members of my church, and in between raising Boer goats outside of town, he volunteered his time to teach and counsel prison inmates, a ministry sponsored by our church. I never saw him without his signature rainbow-colored suspenders, and though I thought him quirky at first, I soon learned that he was a bona fide genius. Genius is often obscured by odd exteriors. Discerning my fragile frame of mind, he offered to talk as friends if I was so inclined. I resisted at first but then agreed to meet, assuming that he would likely take pity and extend emotional support to prop up my plummeting self-confidence. We rendezvoused in a quiet place where I waited for words of commiseration; instead, he shook me to my core: "Get over yourself. You cannot change anyone but you." I fought the angry urge to bolt and run, and what transpired over the course of subsequent conversations saved my life, or at the very least, my sanity. I stopped viewing myself as a victim and learned that grace never leaves me as it finds me; grace flourishes in courageous action. Culture conspires to convince we are powerless against the current of circumstance and the undertow of guilt. Refuse the lie; get over yourself and get on with life. Wounds effect more healing than they inflict damage when we recognize grace at work.

TWO

Influence

The life I touch for good or ill will touch another life, and that in turn another, until who knows where the trembling stops or in what far place my touch will be felt.
—Frederick Buechner

There is a sense in which I have become like those who discipled me—I have become the people I have known and the (authors) I have studied and read.
—M. G. Fray[14]

I slipped quietly onto the back pew in the corner of the narrow whitewashed church sanctuary and settled in for the duration. I came because it was my job as a development officer; we sought to demonstrate respect by attending memorial services of deceased donors, especially for those we had never met. In this case, we received notice that a certain woman had sold some property thirty odd years before, and that she had set aside a portion of the proceeds to benefit my university upon her death. She did not graduate from our school, and no one on our staff had so much as heard of her name, so you can imagine our surprise when we learned of her generous prearrangement. To be honest, I wasn't expecting much. The service began on time with the playing of the Southern anthem "Beulah Land,"

---

[14] M. G. Fray, *It Is Enough* (Georgia: Brentwood Christian Press, 2000).

so familiar that I granted myself mental space to read e-mails on my phone while feigning interest with an occasional upward glance. The pastor stood to speak at the close of the song, and something about the tone of his voice led me to set my phone aside and read the abbreviated bio printed on the backside of the program handout. The country preacher masterfully breathed life into the obituary, followed artfully by strains of "Go rest high upon that mountain. Your work on earth is done." I've heard the recorded voice of Vince Gill at countless funerals through the years, yet it still touches something in me I cannot quite define. I looked across the sea of white, gray, and pinkish balding glare and wondered if the others were thinking about their own nearness to the summit, as was I.

Following the song, the woman's pastor extolled the legacy of the deceased, and with each successive description, I wished increasingly that I had known her. He spoke of her love of books, and her love for the Lord, her children and grandchildren, her church, and nature. He related how that when her health began to fail, she started crocheting coats and hats for the homeless, praying over each item of clothing. The preacher said, "Somewhere in Dallas today there is a homeless person who is warmed by wearing the last hat she ever made. To the earthly end of her ninety years, she lived as one indebted to her gracious Lord." Dying is a distilling of sorts, getting to the root of a life. We think and speak of the essence of a man or woman; details become hazy, and memories take the form of mental snapshots—emotional images frozen in time. What we then live with is the overall impression a person leaves behind, often heralding or dismissing a lifetime with single adjectives: good, bad, kind, loving, harsh, generous—words used at holiday gatherings to recall the missing family member. It seemed to me that this woman's word would be *faithful*, and I couldn't help but wonder what those who know me will use to summarize my life when I'm a yellowing memory.

The following day I was back at home for the weekend, ready to get on with the truly important business of relaxing. The weather was ideal for a great number of things; unfortunately for me, that included raking leaves. My wife and I live among trees, and in the spring, summer, and early autumn, I enjoy them. Our home is surrounded by a panorama of elms, red oaks, pecans, Chinese tallows, and one gangly magnolia. An obnoxious sweet gum and fruitless mulberry, both useless in my opinion, are part of the mix. When these begin to shed their shade, our yard looks like an ocean of leaves, every stiff breeze conjuring up still another amber, gold, and purple wave. Trees may be our friends, but the bottom line is that they leave a mess for me to clean, and this particular Saturday turned into a day of reckoning. Multicolored leaves covered every inch of ground like stippling in a Van Gogh. I enlisted help from next door, and my grandson and I proceeded to rake, shovel, haul, and burn for hours. Exhausted and game called on account of darkness, it seemed like we could have worked for days and be no closer to the goal. There was an end; we simply couldn't see it for the leaves.

Life resembles raking. We exert great effort at doing good—kind words, gracious gestures, helping hands, sacrificial service, *ad infinitum*. Then one day we look up and everything looks the same, so we ask no one in particular under our breath, "What's the point? The bad get ahead, and the good are left behind. Injustice spreads through the world like an incurable rash. Will the madness never end?" The answer is, of course, that it will, for each of us. I cannot speak with certainty on what lies beyond, but I can speak about what remains. Reputation lingers. Acts of grace and mercy outlive us. Buechner writes that love is the frame through which we see our neighbors;[15] I would add that love is a fitting frame for any life. In the end, we are the lasting impression that we leave on the ones we love.

Better to illuminate than merely to
shine, to deliver to others contemplated
truths than merely to contemplate.
—St. Thomas Aquinas

---

[15] Frederick Buechner, *Listening to Your Life* (New York: HarperOne, 1992).

Bumper stickers aren't as prevalent as they were in the '70s, but I saw a throwback on the rear of a Volvo SUV that struck home: "If you can read this, thank a teacher." Come to think of it, for most anything you can do, thank a teacher; however, gratitude rarely flows in the direction of these professionals of transformation. French-born American historian of ideas and culture Jacques Martin Barzun hits the proverbial nail on the head: "Teaching is not a lost art, but the regard for it is a lost tradition."[16] I'll never understand or agree with the inequity in this country that sees teachers on the average make less than plumbers or arborists. In a wonderful coincidence, with the bumper sticker proverb still fresh on my mind, I received a phone call from Ms. Walden, my third-grade elementary schoolteacher. We had only communicated a handful of times since she broke my nine-year-old heart and married someone her own age forty-five years ago, so this was special. What made it even more so was that she called just to say that she was proud of *me*. Amazing! Although she phoned to say that I have blessed her life, the reality is that she is the blessing, having helped to shape my mind and forge my thirst for knowledge into something palpable. No matter how long I live, I will read and think and question in her beautiful shadow.

My first serious attempt at creative writing took place in Ms. Walden's third-grade classroom at G. M. Sims Elementary. The building still stands, but the school no longer exists, having gone the same way as the dodo bird, and my high school for that matter. In fact, the only one of the schools I attended in Port Arthur that is still in use is the junior high that I loathed, although it is now termed *middle* rather than *junior*. Call it progress, poetic justice, or just plain luck of the draw, but the fact that the formative educational spaces of my childhood and youth are long since obsolete makes me feel rather ancient. But I digress. Back in third grade, I wrote a pathetic piece of science fiction that so impressed Ms. Walden that she made an appointment to come to our home and speak to my parents about her promising student, their son. Ms. Walden was beautiful (she still

---

[16] Jacques Martin Barzun, *Teacher in America* (Indianapolis: Liberty Fund Inc., 1981).

is) and had captured my heart by day 2 of the school year, so the thought of her coming to our home was equally exhilarating and petrifying. I was scared witless. I played out possible scenarios like mental chess moves, each of them ending with her in my arms despite the perceived "minor" difference in our ages. The infamous evening arrived; my parents greeted Ms. Walden at our door and ushered her in. They exchanged pleasantries, and at some point in the conversation, my mother came looking for me. I was hiding in my bedroom and not easily found because I had wedged my nine-year-old body as far under my bed as I could possibly fit. Innate timidity trumped romantic love, and I refused to come out until my teacher was ready to leave. My grand opportunity to make a positive impression did not go according to plan, with no one to blame but myself. I received an A+ for writing, but failed my social exam.

My next concerted effort at creative expression came as the result of a different teacher—Ms. Goldman. I will never forget her entrance on the first day of English class my junior year of high school. In she strode, her diminutive five-foot frame stretched erect as a general; she marched silently but swiftly to the blackboard and wrote in white chalk, "Before the high gates of heaven, the gods placed sweat." She then turned and glowered at us, daring anyone to speak, thereby exposing themselves as spineless, lazy, or a combination of the two. We were in for it. She demanded perfection and refused to be what she termed "our crutch"; we were to figure things out for ourselves. Involuntarily at first, I eventually learned from her the enormous power of words and a well-crafted sentence. I promptly went out and purchased my first dictionary and thesaurus from the money I earned mowing lawns. Although I never knew her outside of the classroom, I cannot overstate her importance. Two teachers, as different as daylight from dark, each lingering influences that pull in a positive direction.

In everyone's life, at some time, our inner fire goes out. It is then burst into flame by an encounter with

another human being. We should all be thankful for those people who rekindle the inner spirit.[17]

Am I the only one who tries not to notice the tabloid covers at the grocer's checkout, but inevitably reads a few headlines before swiping my debit card? I gave in again after stopping by my favorite grocer to buy the mandatory K-cups for the next morning's wake-up call. This time, the bold print that lured my gaze was situated next to a photo. It read, "Katy Perry is on fire." I didn't take time to peruse the fine print, but the headline left me considering its meaning. It might indicate an incident of spontaneous combustion; on the other hand, it may be a slang expression meant to describe her pop culture ascension. Either way, the phrase surfaced some timely questions. Just the day before, a former student had posted a fiery comment to one of my blogs: "You were preaching the Kingdom of God with fire when you returned from Kenya & began teaching, preaching, and mentoring at East Texas Baptist University. This memory will last a lifetime!" I'm certain his comment was meant to affirm my relationship to Christ, and although I greatly appreciated the sentiment, the inevitable self-directed question was, "Have I lost the fire?" Does my demeanor still warm those around me and cause others from a distance draw nearer in efforts to catch a spark that will ignite a fire of their own, or have the embers grown cool with time? If so, how would I know? If I *have* lost the fire, can it blaze again?

Life has changed since I stood daily in front of eager undergrads, doing my best to instill appreciation for Bonhoeffer's *Cost of Discipleship*, decipher Bernard of Clairveaux's Four Degrees of Love, and challenging them to join Laubach in experimenting with practicing the constant conscious awareness of God's presence. Life is different. I am different, but has time and distance dimmed the heat? Have pain, disappointment, mistakes, choices, silence, and cultural noise muffled my impact and diffused my influence? Have I forfeited any gifts? Have I settled for insipid convenience and cowered to com-

---

[17] Albert Schweitzer, *Out of My Life and Thought* (Baltimore: John Hopkins University Press, 1998).

fort? While change is inevitable, must spiritual fervor be a casualty to time? There are wounds remaining to be healed and demons that linger, yet brokenness has always been the necessary tinder for spiritual awakening.

The gift I remember most during adolescence was a small wooden plaque my mother gave to me when I was fifteen years old. There was nothing special about the stained and varnished block of wood or the black metal plate attached to the front, but I'll never forget the words etched on its metal surface. Mom wanted to make a point at that impressionable stage of my life, and as usual, she hit her mark (Mom was an emotional sharpshooter). The gift came at what is frequently called a "teachable moment." I remember vividly that I was finding it hard to appreciate my dad and was beginning to vocalize my rebellious spirit. Somehow I lacked appreciation for the man who endured the strained working conditions of an oil refinery worker, welding rail cars and whatever other dirty jobs happened to be required of a boilermaker by trade. Temporary teenage insanity made me forget the sacrifices he had made during my childhood in order to coach the Little League teams I played on, take our family on vacations when paying the mortgage was enough of a challenge, and encourage church attendance even though he never quite understood my passion for church. The gift actually came the day after an uncomfortable confrontation with my father, after which my defiant spirit had reconstructed the incident into fodder for self-pity and still greater defiance. The scene unfurls in my memory like a slow-motion replay: Mom coming home from her part-time job at the Bible Book Shoppe in Port Arthur and placing before me a neatly wrapped package, instructing me to open it. I was confused because it was not my birthday, nor was it any other occasion that would have merited a gift, but I did as she said with one eye on the package and the other on her intense expression. Peeling back the colored paper and removing its tissue shroud, I held the small piece of wood and stared at the plaque. Near the top of the metal plate were etched the letters FOWLKES, and below my surname, I read these words:

> *Son, your father has given you the greatest gift you'll ever receive—his name. He has kept it untarnished for many years, and it is now yours to do the same. Cherish his name as a treasure and wear it proudly. Make sure to never spoil it, so that one day you may pass it on to another who will cherish it just as much.*

Reject the myth of the self-made man; each of us is a collage of influences. I cannot be "just me." We are a divinely stirred mixture of others that imprint us with their own unique reflection of the Triune God. Anything good seen in me carefully resembles my mentors, both the ones I walked with and the ones that continue to mark me by written expression. I love the metaphor a close friend used at his own retirement gala. He humbly and authentically described himself as a mosaic consisting of everyone he had ever known that had positively influenced him. There really is no such thing as "Dane Fowlkes" except in that a name is given to denote this curious montage painted by Henry Fowlkes, Lois Fowlkes, Katie Richey, T. H. Harding, Bill Clark, Bill Malin, Donald Potts, Ira Cooke, Bud Fray, Al Fasol, Vance and Cherry Kirkpatrick, St. Francis, Brother Lawrence, Frank Laubach, Andrew Murray, Oswald Chambers, A. W. Tozer, A. B. Simpson, Henry Blackaby, Frederick Buechner, Stanley Mwongella, and the list goes on. What imprint will I leave upon those who come after me?

†

Do you ever really lose a mentor? My childhood pastor has stepped across to the other side in order to kneel before his Savior and King. T. H. Harding served as pastor of Trinity Baptist Church in Port Arthur from the time that I was in elementary school until some point in my college years. For me, he was larger than life—not in stature, but in spiritual status. He *owned* the pulpit, conveying his own brand of godly swag in vested suits. As he leaned and paced, gesticulated and pleaded, he urged us toward the heart of God. Lifelong lessons are ingrained due to this godly mentor. I learned how to preach by observing and, in turn, imitating him. I know and teach this in leadership development theory as "imitation modeling," but back then, it was more reflex than learned response. One imitates what one respects most, and I have always respected Brother Harding. His passion for Christ and Christ's church infected me with what I hope is an incurable and contagious disease. From him I caught the wind of missions and will forever move with a heart for the nations as a result. He branded my thinking that brokenness is prerequisite for revival; therefore, my own heart whispers a prayer for spiritual awakening in muted tones modeled after the cry of Welsh coal miner Evan Roberts, "Lord, bend me." This I learned from my mentor. What else did I learn from him as a young ministerial student? Instead of asking what I learned about pastoral ministry from Thomas Henry, one might better ask what did not I learn from him? He is missed, but I cannot bring myself to mourn his home going because he is now enjoying what he taught so eloquently as future grace.

†

A room without books is like a body without a soul.
—Cicero

Whenever I'm in close proximity to books, new or used, I cannot help myself. Something otherworldly takes over in secondhand stores, coffee shops—wherever books are sold, and I find myself examining spines, perusing covers, scanning tables of contents, and, more often than not, purchasing. Occasionally I read electronic editions, but nothing replaces the mystery and lure of a shelf lined with volume after volume, beckoning me to unlock their secrets with the key of my mind. I confess that almost as much as I enjoy reading books, I love the smell and feel of them, and all the secrets conjured up by them. I cannot well articulate this magnetic north of literature, perhaps because it's impossible not to think while reading, and equally difficult not to feel. The barren spans of my life are inevitably the periods when I'm not reading.

Books are my friends, and I number among my companions all types of literature, but the genre to which I am most drawn is biography. One of my earliest childhood memories is of spending summers with my mother while she worked among stacks of books. As church librarian, hers was a labor of love, but my experience was anything but work. I thrilled to the rhythm and rhyme of poetry, the uncertainty of mystery, the harrowing escapes of adventure, but my favorite immersion was into the juvenile section and a special edition of biographies written for children. Those orange felt-covered hardbacks contained living documents about real American heroes: Walt Disney, Lou Gehrig, Daniel Boone, George Washington Carver, and others. I quickly developed an insatiable appetite for "story." I did not know then, but believe strongly now, that I am compelled to inhale biography because narrative is always God-breathed. Created in the image of God who lives in perpetual relationship with himself, we are fashioned for relationship. This explains why it is one another's story that grips us and changes our own. Mine is altered in some way by every story I encounter, for better or for worse. Regardless of where I sit in our home, my gaze falls on biographies and autobiographies lining our shelves: Bonhoeffer, Mandela, Franklin, Buechner, Tillich, Livingston, Einstein, Rockefeller, Wesley, St. Francis, Whitier, Tozer, Dinesen, Lewis, Marshall, Merton, Bush, Hemingway, L'Amour, to name but a few. Through ink on vellum, these have been my mentors, teachers, confidantes, comrades, and friends, not so much because of what I have learned about them, but for what they have helped me discover about myself.

†

Technically speaking, it wasn't eavesdropping, but I felt like I had invaded sacred space when I opened the spiral notebook next to the bear-and-fish lamp on the bedside table. We arrived after dark at one of our favorite getaway locations in the Arbuckle Mountains of Oklahoma, where a serpentine assortment of small wooden structures dot a ridge just north of Honey Creek. Our preferred dot is officially designated Cabin #4; it is the second cabin you come to when slowly ascending the narrow gravel drive. The structure itself is less than awe inspiring, but the cantilevered wooden deck overlooking Honey Creek and small but persistent waterfall of several feet down below has climbed near the top of our list of favored short-term retreats. My wife and I have our own accepted duties when settling in to overnight lodging away from home. I unload the vehicle of essential cargo while she arranges sleeping quarters and then tends to kitchen accoutrements. Having completed a couple of trips between Jeep and cabin and properly stowing our limited gear for the weekend, I turned my attention to inside the cabin. I like this place with its mock log interior and exterior, moose and bear pillows, and art prints ruggedly framed and strategically arranged to engender the tenor of a remote bungalow aloft the high lonesome in some wilderness location. Nice try—this is Oklahoma, but I give an A for effort and appreciate the rugged, if not slightly stereotyped, decor.

Beside the queen-sized bed near center stage is a small pine nightstand adorned with only two items. The first is a black metal lamp constructed with a bear holding a fish in its mouth at the base, and topped by a lampshade adorned on four sides by hoofprints that I assume are supposed to be those of a moose. The other is a zebra-print spiral notebook on which someone has written in ink, Cabin #4. It contains personal messages recorded by previous guests, sentiments intended to express appreciation to the owners for pleasant surroundings. I opened the notebook and skimmed through the entries until I came to one dated "4-19-15." It read:

> *I'm not sure who is reading this, but these are my last days. I wanted to be free, hear water, feel air for the last time. Who knows how long we have, but at this very moment I'm gonna live to the fullest and this place feels healing and free. Thank you. Brittany*

A lump formed involuntarily in my throat as it dawned on me that I was reading what well may have been someone's final confession. I turned the page to see if anything followed and found one other entry from Brittany:

> *4-20-2015*
> *Truly, I am still here. Beautiful. Love it. Better than a hospital today. Felt good. I got all the way in the water.... Anyway. I live!!! As long as full as u can. This may be the last getaway I get until the ultimate getaway. Up. Heaven doesn't sound too bad. I love God. I need help, but he will be there. He's here now. Thank you, Brittany*

She had recorded these thoughts six months before, and only God knew if she still lived or if, in her own words, she had made the "ultimate getaway." Either way, her words struck a resilient chord. She had found a way to yell at the top of her pen that she was here; life mattered, and she was part of everything that made sense in the world even when it stopped making sense to her. I closed the notebook, returned it to its familiar place, and sat on the love seat against the wall. Without intending to do so, I said aloud, "Goodbye"; in retrospect, it was more prayer than parting resignation. "It was a long while ago that the words 'God be with you' disappeared into the word goodbye, but every now and again some trace of them still glimmers through."[18] I shut my eyes, prayed for a woman I'll never meet, and asked the Father to enable me to fully live and do so with influence until my own good-bye.

†

---

[18] Frederick Buechner, *Whistling in the Dark: A Doubter's Dictionary* (New York: HarperOne, 1993).

ORDINARY GLORY

I have never been especially impressed by the heroics of people convinced they are about to change the world. I am more awed by those who struggle to make one small difference.
—Ellen Goodman

God reminded me in Cambodia that you can change the world—one prayer at a time. It wasn't as much sudden insight as a slow dawning that rose through every conversation I enjoyed with Christian leaders from across South and Southeast Asia and the Pacific. We shared meals and conversation, but mostly—we prayed. Years ago, Andrew Murray wrote *With Christ in the School of Prayer*; but in Siem Reap, I received an education on how to pray from individuals from India, Nepal, Malaysia, Papua New Guinea, and Indonesia. When these women and men of God address the Father, they clearly expect him to hear and to respond. My own faith frequently falls short, but their confidence in God bolstered my own. The common thread running through all our conversations with one another and with the Father was that God's activity flows in sync with our praying.

In my final time of small-group prayer before leaving Cambodia, I had the enormous privilege of being paired with Jeffrey from Papua New Guinea. I will never forget what Jeffrey requested for each of us. He prayed, "God make us arrows of revival. Fashion us as arrows of destiny." The written word cannot convey the power of that moment; a simple man caught the hem of Christ's garment and refused to let go until he was confident to receive what was requested. I find myself in quiet moments now uttering that same prayer, "God make me an arrow of revival, an arrow of destiny." We can change the world—one arrow at a time.

THREE

Ourselves

This world is a great sculptor's shop. We are the statues and there's a rumor going around that some of us are someday going to come to life.
—C. S. Lewis

Always exceed expectations, especially those you have of yourself.

Grand Avenue is the portion of Highway 80 that runs west and east through Marshall, Texas, but the name is somewhat misleading. Its west end is lined with sagging houses, the old Texas & Pacific Hospital that's been boarded up longer than I've been alive, a *taqueria* leaning next door to a fresh-fish vendor, and the ever-present Dollar General Store. I pulled into town immune to the threadbare surroundings, but couldn't help but notice the barefoot man walking east on the south side of Grand. It may have been the absence of shoes in February that caught my eye, but it was his hoodie that held my gaze. In bold letters on the back, I read:

No Rules
No Master

He appeared homeless, so my knee-jerk response was, "How's that working out for you?" It was likely nothing more than hand-me-down clothing for the man, but who knows? If the bold declaration reflected honest self-assessment, credit him at least with more than a little moxie.

Do I know *myself*? Note that I did not ask, "What do I think about myself?" A world of difference languishes between the two, awaiting the intrepid individual with courage enough for serious self-inventory. Some refuse introspection because they fear a result something like the opening lines to Dostoyevsky's *Notes from Underground*: "I am a sick man. . . . I am an angry man. I am an unattractive man. . . . I'm sensitive and quick to take offense, like a hunchback or dwarf."[19] To the contrary, lives that matter most are the ones who dare to say "I am a sick man," then quickly turn to the physician for the cure.

Many of us whittle away our days stumbling over ourselves. Lacking clarity, we fail to see trees for the forests that loom nearby. Forests are unique to the individual, but each holds potential for revealing trees if we know where to look and are willing to search long and hard enough. "No one longs for what he or she already has, and yet the accumulated insight of those wise about the spiritual life suggests that the reason so many of us cannot see the red X that marks the spot is because we are standing on it."[20] We are tempted to busy ourselves with forests of good things, losing ourselves in the mix, but the wise person wrangles mental space sufficient to consider important questions such as "Who am I?" "What is wrong with me?" "What is right in me?" Such self-awareness may not be politically correct, but is essential to getting at the meaning of grace. Until I honestly face facts—thinning hairline, thickening stubbornness, *et al*—I will never move beyond intellectual assent and dive deep into relishing and reveling in God's unimaginable mercy. Naked self-disclosure cuts and heals all in the same stroke. Honesty is generally painful, perhaps even brutal, but sincere contrition ushers in reparation. The moment I am honest enough to admit to myself the full

---

[19] Fyodor Dostoyevsky, *Notes from Underground* (CreateSpace Independent Publishing Platform, 2016).
[20] Barbara Brown Taylor, *An Altar in the World* (New York: HarperOne, 2009).

extent of my own humanity, I gain a glimpse of God's glory and the wonder of grace. Only those who stumble in the dark fully appreciate the miracle of light. The real difference between those who courageously navigate the narrow way and others who meander aimlessly down side roads is that the former are able to contain their fear long enough to filter from the chaos what is true about themselves and what God can do to make it right. Communing with God is a regular necessity, but there is also a great need for people to take communion with themselves.

†

A wooden cabinet of sorts occupies one wall of the entryway in our house. Situated more for appearance than function, it does, however, sport a full-length mirror that comes in handy for checking wardrobe and hair before heading out for whatever comes next. It is particularly helpful when attempting to force a necktie to hang at the preferred length with its knot bunched just so. I stood in front of the looking glass for its feedback on my appearance, and was relieved that I had done so because a cursory glance revealed that I had missed a belt loop and also that my hair needed more work in the back. Inching closer to the mirror, I found an aging man staring back at me, someone I hardly recognized. Just yesterday I told a senior friend that fifty-six doesn't feel as old as it once sounded. His thoughtful response was, "Give it time." The man I remembered had darker hair and more of it, tighter skin around the eyes, and less of a tire around the middle; diet and exercise are definitely in order—perhaps cryogenics. Regardless, it helps to see things as they are.

Let grace get a good look at you. The more honest you are with yourself about yourself, the more profoundly God is able to knead forgiveness into the essence of your life. Why is it that we tend toward playing Russian roulette with authenticity? Only one moment in six am I entirely present as myself. I waste the rest of my time conjuring up a hologram of what I want others to think of me. What would happen if instead, I allowed others to peak beneath the veneer? What would change if the curtain fell and I stood naked, exposing my thoughts and feelings, hopes and hurts, insecurities and needs? I imagine that many of my relationships would reboot with substance and depth of transformation. Perhaps I am only as good as my next honest question and as real as my succeeding sincere confession.

Self-pity may be the lowest form of disbelief and suffers from selective memory loss. What summons us to find sordid pleasure in self-inflicted lesions—slumbering demons awakened by self-pity? Why contradict grace? Why reopen beleaguered wounds and delay the metamorphosis grace promises? We all have our demons; some have names and faces attached to them, while others are inanimate but no less formidable. The disciple's life is not about eradicating these, but allowing God's love to loosen their hold and God's grace to erase the damning effect when their fiery breath scorches once again. For some, that will sound defeatist. For the most honest, it will ring true and strike an autobiographical chord. I may choose to think my flaws arise from some nether region—"the devil made me do it," but I fear their origin greatly resembles what is deepest inside of me. There is no plot without conflict, and the same must be true for my own narrative. Growth is not possible apart from honest struggle and heartrending hardship, but the difference made by the cradle and the cross is that Christ enters the foray with us. He does not fight the battles for us while we look on disinterestedly from a safe distance; instead, he faces the enemy side by side with us and sways the outcome in our favor. We are more than conquerors because he is in us, and Christ in anyone always adds up to superior force. I will never slay my demons on my own; fortunately, I do not have to.

†

I picked up the game in earnest later in life than I would have if I could start over knowing what I do now. In that way, golf is not unlike a great many things in retrospect—I would choose Boy Scouts over Little League, slide rule over girls, and God's will over my own ego. I do not remember exactly when or where I first saw the game played, but think it was at the old Port Groves Golf Course, affectionately known by locals as the Pea Patch. A few old men hit the course each morning and spent the rest of the day in the makeshift clubhouse playing poker and drinking beer. We termed it a pea patch because it more resembled a garden or abandoned field than a place to play the royal game. Greens varied little from fairways, and fairways were only slightly better mown than the San Augustine growing wildly in "the rough." The only elevation on the course came from the slight rise on the edge of the bar ditch, creating the course's border next to Monroe Street in the Groves.

My father bought a starter set of Northwestern clubs for me and another for himself at Christmas. We played our first round a few days later, and it was so cold that our bargain balls from Woolco cracked and a few even shattered when struck. I survived the arctic eighteen and started playing regularly at the old Pleasure Island course owned by the City of Port Arthur, playing with my best friend after school and every spare minute when we could escape. He was good; I wasn't, but loved every minute on the course and couldn't get enough. In fact, the only time I was ever summoned to the principal's office was for skipping last period my senior year of high school in order to play golf. I purchased a new set of clubs from J. C. Penney after graduation, stowed them in my ample trunk, and set off for college in my '65 Ford Galaxy. Golf was my less-than-magnificent obsession—I played frequently and watched golf on weekends. I wasn't any good, but didn't know or have enough money to take lessons in order to improve. Eventually, I laid aside the clubs and the game I loved, and endured life without golf.

I didn't swing a club for twenty years, until a friend convinced me to pick up the game again. This time around I took lessons and am playing better than ever before, but the real difference is mental. My caddy these days is grace. I strive to improve, but what I want most is to enjoy the moments strung together on the driving range or golf course. I've relieved myself of the awful burden of perfection and embrace the joy of standing on manicured greens and strolling down pristine fairways surrounded by reminders that God is good. Better yet, my wife —a decent player and even better companion— often accompanies me, adding to the glory of it all. I'm working steadily to improve my game, but mostly I am allowing myself to enjoy it. Can I enjoy the game of golf even though I'm not any good at it? Is it possible to love Jesus even though I stumble repeatedly over being salt and light? Allow me to frame it differently: What if discipleship is less about performance, and more about passion? What if Christ-following is more about longing than technical skill? What if the desired end result is not what I am able to produce, but who I become along the way? Grace abounds; joyful are those who revel in and are changed by it.

†

I don't make it by my favorite coffee shop as often as I would like, but that adds to the anticipation and appreciation of the moments when I do. I entered the first time because it was new and only two blocks from where my wife works downtown. I return in part because they serve the best cup of fresh ground coffee in town against the backdrop of great jazz, but primarily because I find myself here. The floors are old—black-and-white honeycomb pattern—a nostalgic companion for the more contemporary brick, wood, and metal accoutrements well suited for a downtown coffee Mecca. I come here to reward myself for nothing in particular, a book tucked under one arm and cell phone at the ready. The place is called Dichotomy because they serve coffee all day and spirits at night, and I find my own dichotomy here—a place to work while relaxing, space to read and think while putting my mind in neutral. Sitting at my favorite table next to an old brick wall covered sporadically by peeling plaster, I easily imagine what it must have been like for writers to gather for debate and creative inspiration in their favorite haunt. C. S. Lewis and the other Inklings met Tuesdays at midday at a local pub called the Eagle and Child, best known in the Oxford community as the Bird and Baby, or simply the Bird. When Hemingway stayed in Venice during the winter of 1949–1950, he spent much of his time at Harry's Bar, where he had a table of his own and often drank with the owner himself.

I am not comparing myself to those literary heavyweights, merely suggesting that we rightly attach meaning to physical locations. It was so from the beginning. Adam and Eve grieved over their exile from the Garden because it was home and because the Creator had walked with them there. Jacob was especially adept at designating sacred plots with names such as "the face of God"[21] and "house of God."[22] Moses piled up rocks to add weight to memories. David went often to his own "house" of God, while longing to erect a sturdy temple to replace the transient tent of meeting. Jesus had Gethsemane and wilderness places in which to retreat, recharge, and, finally, steel his resolve for the ultimate sacrifice. The apostles returned to the upper room to remember who they were until the Holy Spirit could make them what they were destined to be. Everyone needs a place where she or he finds room to dig down deep into themselves, a solitary or perhaps communal context for honest remembering and courageous planning. We face and conquer our fear in sacred space. Call them divine reference points; hope with an address.

☦

Many years ago—more than I care to admit—I made a commitment to God and myself with mostly good intentions (I'm unwilling to claim that I am immune from a selfish motivation here and there). At the time, I called that decisive moment "surrendering to God's call to the ministry" and received profuse affirmation from my faith community and family. I can honestly say that my motives were mostly pure and that I was using vocabulary common to the teaching of my church. All these years later, I understand the fallacy of much of what I expressed that day and believed in the years that followed.

First, the idea of *surrendering* carries with it twin acts of forsaking and relinquishing. In my sixteen-year-old mind, I was turning my back on everything I enjoyed and was good at in order to drag through life the horrible weight of serving Christ. Hopefully, my ministerial penance would merit God's favor. Tragically, no one corrected my thinking and helped me to understand that God created each of

---

[21] *Peniel*, Genesis 32:30.
[22] *Bethel*, Genesis 28:19.

us for a high purpose and that our living out that purpose includes using every God-granted gift and ability for his glory and kingdom advance, while enjoying the adventure of doing so. Instead of surrender, it was more akin to a grand blip on the EKG of discipleship. The Creator intends fulfillment, not rejection. Second, my understanding of "calling" was far too sterile. Somehow I had reached that tender age believing that a divine call could be hoarded by those who served visibly in local churches as pastors, or in foreign lands as missionaries. Surely, only church leaders of the highest profile were carrying out the "high calling." No one helped me discern the threefold aspect of call as presented clearly in Scripture: that every believer is called to salvation, every believer is called to Christlikeness, and every believer is called to ministry—to live out a vocation—doing whatever they do with a strong sense of divine directive. I succumbed to what I now call the "heresy of the definite article." I was mistaken in accepting and attempting to practice pastoral ministry as *the* ministry in the church. Such a mentality leads to anemic churches and burned-out pastors. A superman complex may produce adrenaline highs, but the end result is a low ebb of ministry and even lower trough of long-term spiritual impotence. Rather than relying on what one minister can do, God intends every believer to minister according to her or his various spiritual gifts. Frank Tillapaugh called this interpretation "unleashing the church."[23] I am older now and, I hope, not only wiser but have a better understanding of what God was doing in my life all those years ago and what he continues to do today. I was, am, and will be "called" by God to live out a divine purpose. So too is each of us who follow Christ as Lord.

✝

Everyone thinks of changing the world,
but no one thinks of changing himself.
—Leo Tolstoy

---

[23] Frank R. Tillapaugh, *Unleashing the Church: Getting People Out of the Fortress and Into Ministry* (California: Regal Books, 1985).

I was thoroughly convinced as a younger man that I would change the world. Much older now, I confess I haven't made a dent, except perhaps within myself. I began preaching at the age of sixteen and was pastor of a part-time church by the age of twenty. The Midyett Baptist Church of DeBerry doubled in attendance from four to eight during my eleven-month tenure. Convinced of my pastoral prowess, I moved on to greener pastures where I publicly intended to serve God and privately sought to make a name for myself. I landed in Nacogdoches, where some called me Preacher Boy, a few white-haired widows lauded me the next Billy Graham, and several seniors, covered in calluses and scars from battles with previous preachers, called me names I prefer not to repeat. By God, I was a preacher, and spent the decade of my twenties intent on changing the church. In my early thirties, providence and ambition conspired to take me to the mission field. True to my previous mind-set, I went to Africa fully intent on changing the face of missions. I was, in my mind, the great white hope for the Dark Continent. By God, I was a missionary, and spent my third decade intent on changing the world.

Upon returning to the United States, my alma mater extended an offer I couldn't refuse, and I went to work for the school I loved but from which I'd been estranged due to living overseas. As alumni director and later missions professor and chaplain of the university, I observed ways that we could improve on carrying out our mission, and so I embarked on a plan to bring about those enhancements. By God, I was a Christian educator, and spent my fourth and first half of my fifth decade intent on changing Christian higher education. That crusade has given way to a new challenge as part of the world's foremost international relief ministry. Forty-plus years removed from my initial vision, I understand that my biggest challenge is not to change the world, but to change myself. The most difficult problems to solve are internal; there are depths to plumb because they determine what shows. Daily I'm confronted with the demands of growing in likeness to Christ, gaining the mind of Christ, and in granting others a clear view of Jesus in me. By God, I am a Christ-follower, and my most difficult frontier lies within.

DANE FOWLKES

✝

Jo Beth and I stole away to Louisiana for a few days of genealogical research and rose rustling (taking cuttings from antique roses in order to try and transplant them in our own garden back in Bosqueville), and since we couldn't find a place to stay near Cottonport or Mansura, we resorted to roughing it in a four-star hotel on the banks of the Mississippi River just across from Natchez. Sitting on the banks of what some call the Big Muddy or Ol' Man River, it was easy to feel an odd kinship with Mark Twain; I half expected Tom Sawyer and Huck Finn to come rafting by. Instead of glimpsing rafts and paddle wheelers, I relived childhood pleasures by watching a whitewashed tugboat chug up the Mississippi. As a boy in Port Arthur, we would often navigate our way to the nearby ship channel in order to watch the ships pass. It was cheap entertainment—just the cost of driving ten miles to get there and back—and gasoline was cheap enough in those days. I loved every minute of those quasi-nautical outings and could sit mesmerized for hours, literally watching the world go by. The vessels I most enjoyed were tugboats. I have always felt an odd affinity with these worker ants of the channel—small, compact, useful, one might even say necessary, particularly if you're a barge. These diminutive marine weight lifters are disproportionately powerful, able to do more than one would expect or that it even knows about itself. Tugboats have the character of an English bulldog—Winston Churchill on water; no river royalty for these crafts—leave that for the paddle wheel steamers. Tugs are more akin to river roadies. They do the hard work. There is nothing flashy about them; they go about their aquatic assignments with understated style. Attention inevitably shifts to the bulky but impotent vessel in front that carries the payload, but the crew and well-initiated onlookers know where the credit belongs.

Christian discipleship demands I be a human tugboat, ensuring that Christ gains all the credit for anything good in my life, and content to be a dependable vessel doing the Master's will. Instead of accolades, what disciples need more than anything else is mercy. More times than I can count, I have asked church groups and classes of students which biblical character they would choose to be if they could go back in time. It may surprise you to know, as it has me, that rarely does anyone select the apostle Peter, of all people—spokesman and passionate leader of the Twelve, one of Christ's inner circle, head of the church following Christ's ascension, the Rock for Pete's sake! In considering possible reasons for this anomaly, the best I can come up with is that believers are, for the most part, an unforgiving lot—not primarily of others but of ourselves. We cannot bear to admit our uncanny resemblance to a beloved friend of Jesus who let him down when stakes were the highest. It is hard for us to get beyond the courtyard scene with accusations and sparks flying, Peter swearing, and cock crowing. We fail to acknowledge his stricken heart, grieving and repentant spirit, and dogged determination to never again fail his Lord. Peter struggled with and never fully recovered from his own denial, but the brokenness with which he lived in its wake forged a graceful ethos. Near the end of his life, grace and love became his theme. Exhorting other believers to believe in God's mercy, grace rolled off his tongue as easily as cursing did before.

> *Once you were not a people, but now you are God's people; once you had not received mercy, but now you have received mercy.*[24]

As difficult as it is to believe, it is possible to forgive oneself while remaining sensitive to the conditions that led us astray to begin with. Mercy and memory are suitable companions for disciples. Our most decisive step in magnifying Christ is the one that begins with granting ourselves permission to be forgiven.

†

My grandchildren are convinced that I test-drive rental cars for a living, and that may not be as far from the truth as I would like to argue. I travel extensively for my work, so I've learned how to max-

---

[24] 1 Peter 2:10 (NRSV).

imize my time on the road. As a general rule, I stop by the public library the day before hitting the road and check out an audiobook on CD. I learned early on in my rambling profession that listening helps keep me awake while I drive, as long as the book is a page-turner, so to speak. I was preparing for another development trip but failed to make time to go by the library, so I countered with a contingency plan. On my way out of town, I stopped by Cracker Barrel at the corner of Interstate 35 and Lakeshore Drive because they boast an audiobook rental program in which you pay full price for the set of CDs and receive all but $3.95 upon its return. I am admittedly cheap, so this is not my default approach.

    I loaded the first compact disc and settled back in the driver's seat to listen to *The Book Thief*[25] on my journey eastbound on Highway 31, but was thwarted because disc 2 was damaged. Frustrated and wanting to fill the silence with something beneficial, I tuned in the closest classical music FM station, and it just so happened that the morning's broadcast of *Performance Today* centered upon the story of Leon Fleisher. In 1964, Fleisher's career as a concert pianist was thriving. He had an exclusive recording contract with Columbia Masterworks and was particularly well-known for his interpretations of the piano concerti of Brahms and Beethoven. But then, the unthinkable happened. A seemingly minor accident—a cut on his right thumb—led to a condition called *focal dystonia*, the involuntary curling of his right hand's ring and little fingers. In despair, he refused to shave or cut his hair, and because he couldn't afford a motorcycle, he drove around town with no particular purpose on a used Vespa. He watched his marriage end along with a promising career, until he began conducting, teaching, and playing compositions for the left hand. Forty odd years later, Fleisher was able to ameliorate his *focal dystonia* symptoms after therapy called Rolfing, and experimental Botox injections took him to the point where he could play again with both hands. In 2004, Vanguard Classics released Leon Fleisher's first "two-handed" recording since the 1960s,

---

[25]   Markus Zusak, *The Book Thief* (New York: Alfred A. Knopf, 2007).

entitled "Two Hands," to critical acclaim. Fleisher received the 2007 Kennedy Center Honors.

Sitting on the edge of my seat, literally, enthralled by the dramatic story with a powerful ending followed by a moving recent two-handed performance by Fleisher at age seventy, I couldn't stop thinking about the years during which an award-winning concert pianist was confined to playing with only one hand, and I could not help but draw a parallel to much of my own life. While full of grace and empowered by God's Spirit, I have too often allowed spiritual paper cuts to sideline and render my testimony impotent. An unkind word, unthinking rebuke, a failed attempt, a disillusioning relationship; with relative ease, I hobble myself—a "left-hand only" Christian, an army of one waiting to be unleashed, self-immobilized by pride and disappointment. It is high time to surrender both hands and a whole heart, to do whatever is required to live the "two-handed" disciple's life. Tired of living with one hand tied behind my back, I will accept God's grace, forgive myself and anyone else who has inflicted a cut, and play on with both hands.

†

I saw you outside herding cats in pajamas, so thought I'd stop by for a moment.

My neighbor's statement took me by surprise, as did his uncharacteristic early morning stop on his way to teach at the local community college. I never know quite what to expect from my friend; he is, after all, a musician. As he spoke to me from inside his truck, I stood exposed to the morning in blue tartan plaid lounging pants, college alumni T-shirt, and Joseph A. Banks slippers (I single them out because I'm quite pleased with myself for having found them at a bargain basement price), while our calico and Himalayan played figure eights around my ankles. When our brief conversation concluded and my neighbor headed off to his collegiate destination, my attention turned to the two obnoxious cats, now circling at a frenetic clip. Having acquiesced to their morning demands, I had pause to reflect on my friend's curious phrase, "herding cats in pajamas," and the thought struck hard—that's what I've been doing my entire adult life as a "minister." Vocational Christian ministry is much akin to herding cats, a frustrating divine assignment that leaves the minister entirely exposed and frequently embarrassed. We are exposed because ministry demands transparency or else it is merely play acting. In turn, transparency makes the minister vulnerable to regular criticism and occasional accolades, both of which are damaging to her or his servant spirit. And the payoff—watching cats traipse in figure eights around your ankles while feeling helpless to stop the circus. What would motivate anyone to stoop to such ridiculous servitude? What could possibly enamor enough to seduce one to herd cats day after day and year after year? I can only answer with the phrase the apostle Paul invoked when contemplating his own herd of cats:

Therefore, since through God's mercy we have this ministry, we do not lose heart.[26]

Ministry of any kind is grace.

†

Don't give in to your fears. If you do, you won't be able to talk to your heart.
—Paulo Coelho, *The Alchemist*

We made our annual trek in a rented minivan for family vacation—four adults and three children. On any journey of length, it's helpful if the passengers get along, and fortunately we do, but even for the most congenial and heartiest of travelers, there comes a time for stretching legs and releasing energy. On the second day of our trip, we did just that, making an unscheduled stop in Pensacola, Florida, at the Naval Air Museum. We unfolded ourselves, coaxed legs into action, and walked inside

---

[26] 2 Corinthians 4:1 (KJV).

without knowing what to expect. The cavernous metal building contained different types of aircraft strategically placed to tell the story of flight from Kitty Hawk to the Blue Angels. While our grandchildren quickly rediscovered their land legs in the shadows of every conceivable mode of air transportation suspended by cables from high up metal girders, my wife and I walked at a more age-appropriate pace and attempted to take it all in. As grandparents are won't to do, we looked for ways to maximize the experience for the kids, and our gaze settled on what a sign innocently designated as a flight simulator. With two boys to corral, this seemed just the thing to occupy a twelve-year-old and seven-year-old, the only problem being that the height of the youngest required an adult to accompany them. With their father out of sight pushing their younger sister in a stroller somewhere across the museum, the lot fell to me to ride with them. My wife paid for tickets, and I climbed inside with the boys. I was as anxious as they were for simulated flight until the door closed and I remembered my extreme claustrophobia. Too late to formulate an excuse to exit, it dawned on me that being in a simulator meant that I would be trapped inside a box for who knew how long with no way to escape prematurely with pride intact. While my grandsons laughed and prepared for the "flight," I frantically looked around for a way out and spied a red handle on the ceiling in front of me next to a sign that read Emergency Stop. It might better have been labeled Panic Button. I fought the almost uncontrollable urge to jump up, slam my fist into the red handle, and claw my way out of the crate—I was too young to be buried alive. Instead, I gave myself the pep talk of a lifetime, attempting to convince that the struggle was all in my mind while fighting through cold sweat and gritty panic. The box swayed and swerved in sync with the images on the screen in front of us, and as we slid from side to side, I sat face-to-face with fear. Fear is an ugly thing, especially when it is your own.

What may sound contradictory is that I am unafraid of most things. I do not like snakes, especially a green mamba dangling overhead from a thorny acacia tree while preaching in Tharaka,

Kenya. I have a long-term dislike of the dark forged at an early age, but I am not terrified of shadows. What I do fear is being trapped with no way of escape. It may be relinquishing control, or some other psychosomatic influence, but the bottom line is that fear alters my perception of reality. "We've known for a long time that fear and anxiety can disrupt cognitive processes," says Stella F. Lourenco, PhD, a cognitive psychologist at Emory University in Atlanta. An example is the person who fears losing control over her car because she perceives inclined bridges as steeper than they really are. Again, the mere thought conjures up memories of driving across the Rainbow Bridge near Port Arthur as a teenager. Fear convinces that everything is what it seems to be, even though the perception is far from true.

As the flight simulator heaved and bucked and I fought to regain breath, I remembered something I had read and decided to fling my hopes upon it: "Fear not, for I am with you."[27] A more literal translation is "Do not continue being afraid because I am with you." Fear is conquered by recognizing distortion and then focusing on reality. Face your fear and know that God is working gently behind the scenes to bring you to the light, strengthening you in the process.

> *I was flying somewhere one day when all of a sudden the plane ran into such a patch of turbulence that it started to heave and buck like a wild horse. As an uneasy flyer under even the best of circumstances, I was terrified that my hour had come, and then suddenly I wasn't. Two things, I remember, passed through my mind. One of them was the line from Deuteronomy 'underneath are the everlasting arms,' and for a few minutes I not only understood what it meant, but felt in my nethermost depths that without a shadow of a doubt it was true, that underneath, undergirding, transcending any disaster that*

---

[27] Isaiah 41:10 (KJV).

could possibly happen, those arms would be there to save us if my worst fears were realized.[28]

Fear fabricates an altered state of reality; acknowledging it is a crucial step back into the light of who we are, and, correspondingly, who we are not. View yourself in immediate context as God does, and stride or limp or crawl forward, hand in his.

†

We are apt to make sanctification the end-all of our preaching. Paul alludes to personal experience by way of illustration, never as the end of the matter.
—Oswald Chambers

Beware the danger of putting holiness before God. Pursue Christ. When he shines a spotlight on something that needs correcting, respond to him. Always to him. When he nudges you into course correction, follow him. Never lose Christ in the serving or when attempting to follow his ways. Helen Keller said, "Blindness separates people from things," but when giving undue attention to personal performance, we lose sight of and separate ourselves from *who* matters most.

In the life overflowing in service for others we find God's deep fountain spilling over the spring to find outlet in rivers of living water that bless and save the world around us.[29]

Understanding who I am only becomes important when I see my narrative as helping to write that of others. The whole beautiful

---

[28] Frederick Buechner, *The Eyes of the Heart: A Memoir of the Lost and Found* (New York: HarperOne, 2000).

[29] A. B. Simpson, *The A. B. Simpson Collection* (Kindle Edition: Waxkeep Publishing, 2013).

ordeal reminds that what matters most in the end is not what we have done, but our embrace that speaks of reckless love. The more we make of Christ, the more we resemble him in the process. Like examining baby pictures and debating who the infant most resembles, our lives come into focus gradually if we are astute enough to recognize grace in the commonplace.

FOUR

Community

There is plenty of work to be done here, God knows. To struggle each day to walk paths of righteousness is no pushover, and struggle we must because just as we are fed like sheep in green pastures, we must also feed his sheep, which are each other. Jesus, our shepherd, tells us that. We must help bear each other's burdens. We must pray for each other. We must nourish each other, weep with each other, rejoice with each other. In short, we must love each other. We must never forget that.
—Frederick Buechner

I knew a man who decided enough was enough and abandoned church. He never turned his back on Christ, but although an ordained deacon and amateur biblical scholar, he was unable to justify discrepancies in church leadership and allowed the perceived hypocrisy to drive him away. His retreat became increasingly pronounced and eventually translated into clinical depression that ultimately led him to exit life altogether. Sometime after his passing, his widow gave me a set of biblical commentaries, complete with his handwritten notes in the margins. I've never been able to erase the memory of that devout believer's turmoil resulting in rejection of church.

Church has taken a black eye over the years, but she's given out more than a few of her own. Since no human being is perfect, no group of them will be either; as the song says, "We were made for so much more." We take a hit on our intended identity when we pay more attention to how many attend our services than to how well we love before and after them. I feel sorry for those believers who have never known anything other than the anonymous church. It's hard to experience and express God's love to strangers. Sunday after Sunday in what amounts to the ecclesiastical equivalent of a concert hall, many tread spiritual waters midst a sea of strangers—unknown quantities, mutual anonymity. These are they who look like you, right down to the plaid and khakis, but remain to you a nameless entity, and you a cipher in the snow to them as well. I mourn because you have attended "church" all your life, but have never known the pain and joy of dealing honestly with yourself while face-to-face with a group of people who know the truth but love you anyway. You've probably not encountered the rebuke of teaching on spiritual fullness and then having someone ask, "Well, why then are you overweight?" You have likely never been held by a chain-smoking homosexual who is in the process of coming to Christ but not quite there, and whose scent and searing pain lingers on your skin and in your heart. Odds are you have made it through your church career without wrestling with a church member's addiction, someone you ordinarily would avoid, but, instead, gladly accept her call at midnight in order to go and retrieve her and get her safely to a shelter. I grieve for those who survive a lifetime of Sunday services and Wednesday-night prayer meetings without being more than stirred sporadically and never altered on account of another's narrative.

The reason so many find it hard to go to church is that we have largely lost the notion of what it means to *be* church. We confuse participles for the noun. Singing, praying, dancing, preaching, teaching—these are all but modifiers of the real thing. I enjoy a measure of pageantry and deep down am a person of habit, so I like ritual in worship. I thrill to soul-stirring music. Good preaching always moves me, and bad preaching perturbs me (not to say I haven't done my fair share of it). But all these may be experienced alone and in private. What makes church, *church,* is that I am present with other pilgrims, connected physically as well as spiritually. It is relationship that morphs routine into corporate worship; me loving you, and you loving me, liberates both of us to love and worship God. Absence does not make the heart grow fonder; it cools and dulls the spirit. This is not a new problem. One particular church in the New Testament was having a dickens of a time getting folks to show up, hence the admonition:

> *Not forsaking the assembling of ourselves together, as the manner of some is; but exhorting one another: and so much the more, as ye see the day approaching.*[30]

✝

I endured a more than a difficult week that reached a painful climax. My position and responsibility caused me to make an excruciating choice that was, to say the least, gut-wrenching. The thing about wounds is that they leave scar tissue behind whether or not the original cut remains visible, and generally the knife cuts both ways. We may take great care to appear unscathed, but in reality, most of us are both the walking wounded and source of someone else's hurt. In the aftermath of the ordeal, one of my supervisors remarked, "It would be a perfect job if it wasn't for having to deal with people." I instantly felt a pang of guilt because I have heard myself say the same thing in the past about churches, as if any number of people haven't thought or said the same thing about me: "Church would be a great place if it wasn't for the preacher." What is it that turns church into a cruel joke, or worse, a harmless cliché? I love the church; it is certain churches I have a problem with, yet I've spent my life serving these imperfect organisms. I'll admit that she is frequently her own worst enemy, and refuse to blame anyone for rejecting her dark side. I've fantasized about walking away myself never again to darken her gothic doors, or sit another Sunday in light diffused by stained glass, or homilize another Lord's day from behind a well-oiled oaken pulpit; however, I always return because I need her. More to the point, I

---

[30] Hebrews 10:25 (KJV).

need *you*. You are able to see God at work in me when I cannot feel or hear or see him hanging around; grace means that I return the favor. Like it or not, we need one another.

Granted, there are issues. The proliferation of both government services and parachurch organizations are an indictment against the church; they flourish when she fails. More than a few high-profile churches have become big business in the effort to lure large crowds, as if attendance is her *raison d'être*. Concert Christianity trumps discipleship at every turn, and we aren't even aware that we are skating on thin ice; spiritual DNA is forfeited for cheap imitations. Spiritual sideshows lead us to believe it's harder to live like Jesus at church than anywhere else. Christians appear to work less at getting along than those who claim no connection to the church or Jesus; I will never cease to be amazed at the way we treat one another in the name of Christ. Is it any wonder that the masses are either turning away or staying away from church? Who can blame anyone for choosing not to be the brunt of someone else's critical spirit, even if that less-than-exemplary spirit is displayed in Jesus's name. There is more good-natured camaraderie and *joie de vivre* at the corner pub than in many churches, and I cannot help but wish that church more resembled Alcoholics Anonymous than the Friday Night Fights. What most are seeking is an accepting group of individuals who love without judgment or condemnation. I hang on to the slim hope that this may one day be found at church.

Having admitted our dark side, I hasten to remind myself that the disciple's life was always intended as dialogue, never monologue. In many ways, some I'm proud of and others that I'm not, I am the product of churches I've known and been a part of, and I am different in a good way because of the church I now consider home. We are imperfect because human beings never are, and I should bite my tongue the next time I am tempted to say church would be a perfect place if it wasn't for people. Grace is eminently practical. One example of its relevance in ordinary circumstance is how grace instructs and empowers me to deal with "irregular people" (my wife's clever phrasing). Yes, there are some who grind on my nerves like grating Parmesan cheese, and I imagine that the feeling is mutual; however,

ORDINARY GLORY

I find it entirely possible on the basis of God's grace to fully forgive, refuse bitterness, and refrain from criticizing, even though I may still not like someone or prefer to be around them. Not quite as easily, grace empowers me to forgive myself, even though at times I'd prefer to be anyone but me. Whether I am learning to forgive someone else or to pardon myself, God's grace is the touch point that changes everything.

✝

Our community is quaint in much the same way an outdated custom is remembered with a smile and promptly disregarded for more fashionable ways, but by and large, we like it that way. I headed home from three taxing days on the road and started to relax once I turned onto Steinbeck Bend, embracing the warmth of familiarity as I dipped down and through the low water crossing on Rock Creek Road en route to my own micro-universe on Private Road. The outside world intrudes now and then with stark reminders of mortality and gray morality—the importunate cancer that shadows the steps of a good neighbor, an older couple in our church arranging to adopt a prematurely birthed grandchild because their daughter is losing her battle with substances beyond her control, our own daughter foster parenting with a powerful sense of divine directive to rescue children from appalling environs and hopeless futures. We are not immune to the world's distress or moral desolation, but we endure each together.

Our mailing address reads *Waco*, but those of us who live here or travel to church nearby from outside of the area refer properly to our home as Bosqueville, an ironic order of things in light of the little known fact that Bosqueville predates Waco and, prior to the Civil War, dominated the region with its cotton farms, gin, and three colleges. Landmarks in our community are rather sparse these days—an elementary, middle, and high school; modest football field and faded aluminum bleachers; three little league fields; three churches; an historic cemetery; and a now defunct feed mill situated around the S-curve and up Rock Creek from my house. Life happens in some and is remembered in others, but each stands as a monument to the weight of glory in honest sweat and divinely infused human effort. The most enduring markers are the families that nurture one another, grieve together, and see God's grace in each other's lives. We are not stumbling along some predetermined path or making it up as we go, but learning that life is intended to be endured and embraced in the company of others.

I live here because my wife lived here before me, and over the past ten years, I have grown not only accustomed to these surroundings, but to care for the people who are fixtures in them. Two such residents who mean a great deal to me are our landlords and neighbors from down the simple country lane I now call home. This relationship led to my agreeing to preach for a time at their small historic church, which stands near the geographical gateway to the modest region. The white clapboard church building wears the label Methodist, but consists of parishioners who are primarily not Methodists—a denominational Heinz 57. In an oddly unpredictable way, I fit—in this church, in this community, in this home. I've been thinking lately that if you were granted an opportunity like the one given Karen Blixen by Denys Finch Hatton in *Out of Africa* as she flies in an open cockpit biplane over her beloved Ngong Hills, you would peer down over the side and notice a quiltlike pattern spread out below you, a fitting image for a quilting people. Like the land, we are pieced together here like gingham patches in an antique quilt. In the overall scheme of things, not many have lived and died here over the past one hundred and sixty years. The cemetery reveals as much about this community as anything living. A relatively few familiar family names are etched in stone, scattered throughout Bosqueville cemetery like a circling of the wagons, a community's last stand against the onslaught of life and death. In the end, Bosqueville cannot be understood by GPS coordinates or surveyor's stakes; it is defined by its residents. The community persists along family lines, where neighbors know one another, attend each other's funerals, and applaud one another's children at school celebrations and athletic contests. This is not a place for strangers. It is a place for friends, family, and, above all else, it is a place for being known. God intends his churches to be just that—places for knowing and being known. We were created for him and to live in relationship with him and each other, a community in the fullest sense of the word.

Most Sundays, my wife and I are a part of two vastly different faith communities. One of them has stood in this community since 1853, but my wife and I are newcomers. To be honest, I wonder at times if it makes any difference at all that I'm here (and I'm the preacher), but then look around and remember why it is important that I am and that anyone else would be too. There is a young man on one side of the sagging sanctuary holding a little girl who isn't his child, but she clings to him like he belongs to her. There's a man my age who was just released from jail, flashing me a victory sign as he enters. In the vestibule stands an older woman who sees life differently since her stroke, waiting to hug me and give the same greeting from her sister she gives at least twice every Sunday morning. To my left is the older man who lost his wife a few years ago and finds his purpose in life these days by tending the climbing roses in the prayer garden. Standing in the choir is the sweet rancher who silently mourns every Sunday that she can do everything with her weathered husband except attend church. Over there is the bent and largely hairless woman who has helped so many others through times of crisis, now waging her own battle against the onslaught of cancer. We are all different, but each Sunday morning, we celebrate what we hold in common. It is for this reason I find the church growing on me, and not like an unwanted mole that rouses suspicion for cancer. My wife turned to me one morning on the way home from worship and said, "You're a good fit for this church." She meant it as a compliment, and I took it as the same, but must confess that I was not so sure from the outset of our sojourn here. We are an eclectic blend. I cannot remember knowing and counting myself part of a more disparate collection of individuals, but our differences provide a clear view of grace in relief. Highly educated and largely uneducated recite the Lord's Prayer with one voice, cowboys and city slickers kneel near one another on the same maroon velvet altar, women and men stand on equal footing before the Lord and the church, and young children pass the collection plates to the elderly each Sunday. One of my favorite moments in worship comes just after the offering as we stand to sing the doxology. I choke back emotion while the nine-year-old usher to my right, who comes from a less-than-ideal home environment, sings out at the top of his voice, "Praise God from whom all blessings flow!" I love this menagerie; what's truly amazing is that they love me in return.

Sunday evenings find us in a very different setting. For half of the years I've lived in this small community, we have been part of an even smaller community of faith. While some would describe it as a house church, we might more accurately be described as a studio church, since we meet most Sunday evenings in Runnin' Bird Studio. The recording studio belongs to our friends across Private Road, and they have welcomed us into their musical sanctuary and their lives for so long now that we consider each other family. We are an eclectic lot; on the surface, one would say we hold nothing in common, yet we have adopted one another as extended family. We call ourselves church because we are a prophetic community of faith; prophetic in the sense that we are a positive change agent in the community, and we experience community in that we relate to one another on a foundation of trust. We refuse an inferiority complex because we demonstrate the importance of worshipping and serving with those we know. In other words, strangers may attend an event together and even sit in a pew next to one another, but relationship is required in order to be church. Trust is only given to those we know. Finally, there is faith. The church must live out moment by moment a radical relationship with Jesus Christ; otherwise, we are nothing more than a low-budget social club with high-maintenance members. We are to be defined by him more than we are by each other, by place, or by effect. Here's the kicker—all three elements must be active in order to be church. Failure at any point negates the whole. Such an understanding places no importance on size and gives no weight to demographics. What it does stress emphatically is that being church means to be transformed from the inside out by an intimate relationship with Christ.

†

ORDINARY GLORY

Walmart changed my life, or this portion of it anyway. I innocently entered Walmart, prepared to wait for my wife while she checked out holiday leggings for our granddaughters. It had already been a long day of work in addition to 18 brisk holes of golf in a 40-degree chill and dinner out with family, so I determined to sit this one out on a metal bench near the sliding-glass exit doors. The pause quickly transitioned into people watching like I do when waiting for a flight in a busy airport terminal, and a line from Walden popped involuntarily into my thoughts, "The mass of men lead lives of quiet desperation." In a fifteen-minute span that seemed more like an hour, I saw adolescents trying to look like older persons, and old people trying desperately to look young, neither of them a pretty sight. I heard at least five different languages being spoken, and one of them may even have been English. Every size and color of humanity paraded past, but what grabbed my attention were the eyes that spoke of resignation without ever speaking. "Alas for those that never sing, but die with all their music in them."[31]

One elderly heavyset and snowy whiskered man in particular commanded my attention. His blank expression and empty eyes stood out from underlying bags like hard-boiled eggs. Were you to look up the word *lost* in the dictionary, you might expect to see his face staring blankly back at you. He did not appear to be homeless, but I began to worry about him because he moved slowly in an aimless four-foot circle, obviously unable to decide what to do or where to go next. I weighed my options. What social services could I call? Should we just take him home until able to locate next of kin? Perhaps this was a job for the authorities and I should notify the police. While fingering 9-1-1 on my phone, my wife approached the checkout and motioned for me. She wanted my opinion on the leggings, so I used one eye to examine leggings while keeping the other on Mr. Lost in Space. I was incredibly relieved when a woman

---

[31] Richard A. Posner, ed., "The Voiceless" from *The Essential Holmes: Selections from the Letters, Speeches, Judicial Opinions, and Other Writings of Oliver Wendell Holmes Jr.* (Chicago: University of Chicago Press, 1997).

approached, took the man by hand, and left the store with him. He wasn't lost after all, at least not for the time being.

It started like the nagging of a song that you know you know but can't recall the words of or tune. It was emotional, but more than emotion; thought-provoking, but more than a notion. On the way through the parking lot to our Jeep, I finally recognized it. This was the voice of God speaking through the piercings and tats, addressing me midst the cacophony of languages, age and gender confusion, plethora of empty eyes, and elderly men walking around in circles. The voice said, "They are confused and helpless, like sheep without a shepherd." Along with the message came a gentle reminder that I bear enormous responsibility for these wandering lambs. I teach that as Christ-followers, our commission is to point as many as possible toward the Good Shepherd, but had personally lost this perspective and corresponding sense of urgency. Over time, I had allowed calluses to form on my heart causing me to view these as misguided nuisances rather than desperate and dying human beings. I have far to go in reclaiming the heart of Christ, but this Walmart reminder has pointed me in the right direction.

†

Why read a book, visit an art museum, attend a play, listen to a symphony, or make time to watch PBS? The answer is more profound than one might expect—so that you will dare to get your hands dirty, have your mind sharpened, spirit quickened, understanding broadened, or sense of humor restored. You may never lift a brush or strum an instrument, but you are better as a result of those who have, if you position yourself in the flow of their genius. Marjorie McCoy called this "secondary creativity," and Tillich had this to say about it: "In order to be spiritually creative one need not be what is called a creative artist or scientist or statesman, but one must be able to participate meaningfully in their original creations.

Such a participation is creative insofar as it changes that in which one participates, even if in very small ways."[32]

The same process is in play when I rub shoulders with those who are smarter, better, or more spiritually savvy. I am made a better and brighter person because of my exposure to what God looks like inside and outside of others. Even as a mirror helps me recognize myself, I comprehend more clearly what God is erecting in me by viewing what he is constructing in fellow pilgrims. He comes into focus every time I hit golf balls with my ex-offender friend, sit with an octogenarian widower whose robust health is failing for the first and last time, overhear the struggles of a seminary graduate describing the dearth of spirituality, watch a friend work past scars from a domineering mother, and discern grace in the eyes of my wife. Left to myself, I tend toward smallness, spiritual inbreeding in which everything I become is a little less than what I was before; I need others if I am to permit God to save me from myself.

This may not seem to make sense, but much of the Christian experience is nonsensical in a postmodern world. The kingdom of God may best be described by the theological term *topsy-turvy*, which comes in handy when ordinary words fail to capture the essence of a moment or the import of a movement. First recorded in England in 1528 as a compound word formed from *top* and the obsolete *terve*, meaning "topple over," *topsy-turvy* portrays the sense of confusion one feels when things are not in proper order or are metaphorically upside-down. That is more or less what Jesus meant when he said, "My kingdom is not of this world."[33] He was reminding us that earthly kingdoms are not identical to the kingdom of God, a fact frequently lost on church leadership. Rather than standing in relief or opposition to these kingdoms, Christianity has often imitated them and is still hard at it. A modern trend is afoot to redefine the pastor as CEO, the church as a corporation, parishioners as customers, and to judge the whole ecclesiastical kit and caboodle according to a numer-

---

[32] Quote by Paul Tillich, included in Clive Hazell's *The Experience of Emptiness* (AuthorHouse, 2003).

[33] John 18:36 (KJV).

ical bottom line. This obsession to imitate Madison Avenue explains the popularity of prosperity theology and edges the church precipitously toward the abyss of conformity. According to this scenario, the Gospel is more akin to a good stock tip, or picking the right horse at Louisiana Downs, or lucking out with the right number in the lottery, than it is to changing the world. "The righteous get rich and the poor get what they deserve."[34]

The consistency with which the kingdom of God is not the opposite of the kingdoms of the world should serve as a warning to us. Donald Kraybill suggests that "the kingdom of God points to an inverted, or upside-down way of life that contrasts with the prevailing social order."[35] Jesus of Nazareth was well versed in topsy-turvy theology. Speaking to some rudely religious people, he warned: "I tell you the truth, the tax collectors and the prostitutes are entering the kingdom of God ahead of you."[36] He shocked his disciples by saying, "It is easier for a camel to go through the eye of a needle than for a rich man to enter the kingdom of God."[37] Before we shout amen too loudly and continue on about our business, it would behoove us to repent from acting like Christianity is a status rather than a calling, for downplaying the responsibilities of a relationship with God and only emphasizing its benefits. No wonder so many are rejecting the church—if the church is not committed to changing the world, it has become irrelevant. "Thy kingdom come, Thy will be done on earth as it is in Heaven" must move from being a prayer to becoming our vow.

†

---

[34] James Mulholland, *Praying Like Jesus: The Lord's Prayer in a Culture of Prosperity* (New York: HarperOne, 2001).

[35] Donald Kraybill, *The Upside-Down Kingdom* (Harrisonburg: Herald Press, 2011).

[36] Matthew 21:31 (KJV).

[37] Matthew 19:24 (KJV).

Others look for reasons to shop; I find that any excuse will do so long as it takes me to a library. In that spirit, I stopped by Waco's Central Library to return a book, and although I could have placed it in the drop slot provided for just that purpose and left, I convinced myself that I could actually enter and confine my browsing to a minimum. I saunter through aisles of books like a connoisseur swirls and then inhales the aroma of vintage wine. All libraries and bookstores hold a certain attraction, but this is especially sacred space for me. Before securing a hotspot for my iPhone, Central Library was the most convenient place for me to access free Wi-Fi, so it became for a time, in effect, my office. Appearances have changed a good deal since those days. A major renovation by the City of Waco netted a fresh coat of paint, altered design, updated furniture, and expanded holdings. The one constant is its clientele. Seated in front of every computer screen and on every lounging chair in every remodeled nook and cranny is a colorful array of ragamuffins, homeless persons. Jokingly, I've remarked that our city has the most highly educated vagrants around. Seriously, sitting next to and interacting with them over time gave me a deep appreciation that went beyond the sights and smells that conjure stereotypes. To this day, I call them my peeps.

Walking through the library's blacktop parking lot to my vehicle, I spotted a penny on the ground and hovered over it, uncharacteristically debating my response. I imagined faint whispers of my wife's voice reciting her common response to such an innocuous find, "Positive cash flow." Ordinarily I retrieve coins of any denomination, harkening back to childhood discoveries. Fifty years ago, it would have thrilled me to find a penny on the ground, and I would have rejoiced all the way to my piggy bank, although it wasn't a piggy bank at all, but a small black box with a slot on top to hold a coin. As soon as you inserted the coin, a glow-in-the-dark hand magically emerged to grab the coin and jerk it inside (my father's preferred alternative to traditional children's banks). Finding unexpected cash is always pleasant, although in my case, monetary discoveries normally consist of currency found hiding in pockets that I absentmindedly abandoned some time before, hence negating the idea of positive cash flow; chalk my "finds" up to recirculation. However, for reasons I cannot explain or defend, I chose not to pick up this particular penny and take it to the bank.

Fast-forward to navigating Champion Forest Drive in the Champions region of Houston the next day just after a toad-floater downpour. As I slowed to a stop near the intersection of Champion Forest and Farm to Market 1960, I spotted a middle-aged man portside holding a small cardboard sign that read: Pennys Help (misspelling is his, not mine). We rarely see such sign-bearers at intersections in Waco, but when I do, I typically lower my window and make a token offering if I have cash on hand (which, quite honestly, I seldom do). More frequently, I offer to take the individual to buy something to eat, and the panhandlers take me up on the offer about thirty-three and a third percent of the time. On this occasion in rush-hour traffic, on an already jam-packed artery, I did neither. I did not lower my window, nor did I offer assistance of any kind. I merely read the handwritten sign as I passed: Pennys Help. Arriving at my destination shortly thereafter, I had about twenty minutes until my next appointment, long enough to consider the juxtaposition of the two unrelated, yet oddly similar, experiences. In both cases, something of value stood within reach, but I chose to ponder and then pass by. The value of both was deemed too small to warrant my involvement.

The unexpected ethical confrontation reminded me of the time I chose to go undercover as a homeless man on the streets of Waco in order to get inside their heads if not under their skin. I convinced myself that I would never represent Christ with convincing compassion if I had no clue what it is like to walk the streets without knowing what I will eat or where I'll sleep. My wife was less than enthusiastic about the decision, but one hot summer day, I donned my dirtiest T-shirt, oldest shorts, most ragged shoes, and drove downtown. I parked my pickup on the edge of downtown, locked my wallet and cell phone in the truck, and set out for only God knew what. It was important to me to spend a couple of days penniless and communicationless, but I quickly learned that it would be no picnic—heat, humidity, and hunger make for a formidable trinity of want. I stopped by the local homeless ministry to inquire about a place to stay the night and learned that to do so, I would need to shower along with the other transient men. I acquiesced to the requirement, accepted a towel and complimentary toiletries, and must admit that I felt my dignity drip slowly from me along with the cold water in the primitive surroundings. I learned that finding a free drink of water downtown in one hundred–degree heat is a job in itself, and by the evening, I slumped nearly dehydrated and heat exhausted onto a rusty folding chair inside a Lutheran church that provides a free meal to the homeless every Tuesday night. I honestly cannot say what made more of an impression—the spaghetti and bread that I gulped down like a starving man, the ice tea that rehydrated me, or the volunteers that remained resolute behind the four-by-eight-foot tables, as if plastic could shield them from the pain and need that filed dejectedly in front of them. I listened to a preacher wax generically about hope, but my mind kept wandering to where I would rest my depleted body that night. In short order I experienced an odd camaraderie with a homeless band of brothers, as well as the shock of having people cross streets to avoid me, the majority refusing to look me in the eye. As parched as I remained those summer days, I soon found my greater thirst was for human dignity. I will never look at or fail to look upon the "least of these" as before. I listened to profound stories of human agony and shattered dreams, saw raw expressions of thinning hope; most of all, I gained a heightened sense of the importance of speaking a name, the significance of daring to touch, and the magnitude of grace. There is no end to human variables; the constant is God's love. Grace refuses to force individuals into a mold cast for someone else; the Gospel of Christ is a narrative of grace, custom fit for each story. The truly Good News is that God knows *me*. He's acquainted with my story; in fact, he is helping to write it. Grace finds me wherever I am and speaks a language I understand. Grace never requires me to imitate anyone other than Christ.

The apostle Paul has something to say about the value of others in an autobiographical account that leads to a remarkable declaration.[38] He describes an impressive and impeccable religious pedigree,

---

[38] Philippians 3:1–11.

then marks it all null and void in light of the greater value of knowing Christ. His own study in contrasts leads us down the path to deeper intimacy with Jesus Christ. Essentially, religion is revealed to be inferior to relationship. The apostle Paul wrote as he was moved by the Holy Spirit, but that did not hobble him from expressing ideas at times that confound the smartest among us and dismantle the most self-assured. One such statement is, "Look not only to your own interests . . . Consider others better than yourselves."[39] I barely pull myself from survival mode long enough to acknowledge anyone else, much less prefer their interests to my own. When I pretend to do so, my words ring tinny and hollow, and even a bat could see that I am disconnected from my heart. Is Paul encouraging us to paint the clown's face and pantomime love? Are we to fake it with the hope that we will eventually deceive ourselves into accepting our pasty makeup as our real face? I am convinced the aged apostle has something much more authentic in mind. Paul does not encourage low self-esteem but "no-self esteem." When I begin to recognize and genuinely believe that what others need and want is as important as my own needs and wants, theirs become more important than my own, and I have traveled a long way down the road of actually losing sight of myself.

†

All the world is full of suffering. It is also full of overcoming.
—Helen Keller

Huddling by candlelight is not necessarily romantic. My wife and I reclined on pillows in the inky hallway because Mother Nature was taking a howling swipe at us. Although definitely not the right setting for romance, it would have at least been peaceful were it not for our neurotic dog. Misha has been a member of our family for only a few months, but is already ensconced as a couch potato of the high-

---

[39] Philippians 2:4 (NIV).

est variety. My wife gave her to me on my fifty-sixth birthday, and we both marveled at the time at her ridiculously low price. Registered Rhodesian Ridgebacks normally sell for a thousand dollars or more, making Misha's $100 price tag a mere pittance. Born six years ago, she has been used for breeding all her life, and the story we were told is that her fifth and last pregnancy was brutal. None of the litter survived, so her breeders were looking for a home where she would be well cared for and loved. The three of us meshed almost immediately, but my wife and I have since gained a better understanding as to why Misha was not strong breeding stock. Our first clue came during a deafening thunderstorm. Misha paced back and forth panting, then attempted to wedge her seventy-two-pound frame into the two-foot space behind my wife's embroidery table. The second clue materialized as we watched Misha react in abject terror when she encountered our cats. Ailurophobia is not a desirable trait for Ridgebacks originally bred by Afrikaaners for the purpose of hunting lions. Suffice to say that a breeding dam afraid of her own shadow comes up short in the desired DNA department. Daughter of Simba and Nala, granddaughter of Sidboarani Ruffion Muskit Ridge, great-granddaughter of Zyon King of Kalahari, Misha Kalahari is an adorable companion, but a lousy champion of canine ferocity.

The image of Misha cowering before our Siamese and calico came to me the other day when I caught myself relinquishing hope in the shadow of towering concerns. Created in the image of the Almighty and recreated by the resurrected king of kings, how is it possible to succumb to the weight of worry and fear? Vocal minorities and savvy political charlatans claim the upper hand, all the while powerless to overcome the One who has already overcome. A defeated believer is an oxymoron; Christianity was never intended as defensive posture. Jesus says as much when he declares that the gates of hell will not prevail against his church. The better translation of "the gates of hell shall not prevail" in Matthew 16 is "shall not withstand." The church marches relentlessly forward, and the forces of evil cannot withstand her onslaught.

> *Think about the picture here. Jesus says the gates of hell will not prevail against the church. Now tell me, how do gates prevail? When have you ever seen gates on the march? They don't attack. They fortify. They are there to hold their ground. That's all. Hell is not on the offensive, brothers and sisters. The church is on the offensive. The church is marching into all the hells in this world, ready to reclaim every square inch for Christ. And when we storm the gates of hell, Christ promises that we cannot fail.*[40]

Make no mistake about it, we are at war. "Moral relativity is the enemy we have to overcome before we tackle atheism" (C. S. Lewis). The great news about the Good News is that believers are in the battle together and we are on the winning side.

---

[40] Kevin DeYoung.

FIVE

Worship

> *Human beings may separate things into as many piles as we wish—separating spirit from flesh, sacred from secular, church from world. But we should not be surprised when God does not recognize the distinctions we make between the two. Earth is so thick with divine possibility that it is a wonder we can walk anywhere without cracking our shins on altars.*
> —Barbara Brown Taylor[41]

My childhood landscape included humidity-stained concrete, manicured San Augustine lawns, and cement asbestos siding houses on one end of Lay Avenue with brick homes on the other. Hurricane-force winds regularly altered the landscape, replacing shingled roofs with blue tarpaulins. We grew as accustomed as one can to the odor of rotten eggs, which became more pungent at night when darkness shrouded toxic emissions from nearby petrochemical refineries. Shrimp was king in Port Arthur with crawfish a close second, and both were seasonally available fresh from the Gulf right out of white Styrofoam coolers in car trunks on the side of many roads.

Even more memorable was the spot that fueled my imagination more than all others and triggered emotions still not fully cata-

---

[41] Barbara Brown Taylor, *An Altar in the World: A Geography of Gaith* (New York: HarperOne, 2009), 15.

logued—a small stand of oak and pecan trees standing in relief from concrete surroundings, guarding the passageway between houses on Franklin Avenue and a large grassy field behind Doctor's Hospital. This cluster of deciduous sentinels formed what became a secret clubhouse for me, Kurt, Mitch, Xavier, and the other boys living on Lay Avenue. It was Sherwood Forest, Camelot, 221b Baker Street, the Bat Cave, World War I squadron headquarters, or any other setting conjured forth from adolescent imagination. It was a holy place, space where I strongly sensed the presence of God, where he was beautiful to me and where I learned that nature and imagination catapult a powerful turning to the Creator. I still pray more naturally out-of-doors than inside any constructed cathedral. I attempted to return to this sacred space a number of years ago when introducing my wife to my childhood haunts, but found that the grove had been cut down and paved over, a magical forest reduced to generic asphalt. What remains, however, cannot be removed, because it lives on inside my thoughts and serves to remind that the Holy One is not opposed to meeting us in earthly spaces.

Worship is awareness, not activity. When understood in reverse, the focus of worship shifts to the act or its environs rather the Lord God Almighty himself. Herein lies the terrible crux of so-called worship wars. When battling over modes of worship or styles of music, we march proudly away from God's presence and slink into incipient self-worship. Attention shifts from the Creator onto creature comfort—our own fervor, loudness, posture, musical preference, or any number of other details that place us at the center of the universe. Scripture offers a multitude of worship postures and expressions, but never loses sight of Holy God. Worship is always reaction rather than initiation—I see God, hear him, know he is near; therefore, I respond to him. Worship as initiation is idolatry and always produces preoccupation with form rather than substance.

†

Thus the heavens and the earth were finished, and all the host of them. And on the seventh day God

> *ended his work which he had made; and he rested on the seventh day from all his work which he had made. And God blessed the seventh day, and sanctified it: because that in it he had rested from all his work which God created and made.*[42]

Worship is as much about resting as it is concerted effort. I am admittedly no expert on relaxing, but I am a willing apprentice. My work ethic stems from a boilermaker father and industrious mother. Both parents gave their best, saved what they could, and forged a safe place from which a son and daughter could try their wings. Life was framed by how hard one worked, but one thing Henry and Lois insisted upon was family vacation every summer and to take it easy on Sundays. Without digging deep into the why of it, they went with the instinct that great effort can only be sustained if punctuated with a little downtime. Our Creator established the pattern of hard work and consistent rest, knowing that without periodic relaxation and frequent solitude, stress takes its toll, leaving life ragged and in danger of unraveling. Take a deep breath. Hold it. Release it, slowly. Sometimes stress relief comes from intentional inactivity—retreat, renew, refresh. At other times, intrepid action is required. Allow no bitter root to take hold of your heart. Resolve disputes. Apologize for hurt. Repair broken relationships. Restore what has been taken or lost. Retreat from distraction, no matter how hard you have to work to get away. Rest is not for the faint of heart, but it does the heart more good than any medicine.

Solitude is a state of mind, not merely the absence of noise, and it forms a fitting backdrop for recognizing and connecting with Almighty God. My wife summoned me to our back porch in order to witness the spectacle of migrating hummingbirds, a myriad of ruby-throated and black chins, diving and dueling, making quite a clatter in the process. We were granted ringside seats to a rare and powerful display, and in that moment, solitude ran rampant over us as we witnessed the handiwork of God. Anyone who stands outside long

---

[42] Genesis 2:1–3 (KJV).

enough after sunset encounters the night symphony of the Creator. Nature does not make noise; nature produces music. Insomniatic insects fill the night with music that has a primal rhythm to it.[43] Each scratch or thrush or squeal or hum is not out of place; in fact, such nocturnal sounds remind that life is consistent and patterned. God is always speaking, but only those who exert the effort to be still can hear him. Solitude is an attitude of heart that allows space to discern the Creator, and, in time, ourselves.

☦

> *What can we gain by sailing to the moon if we are not able to cross the abyss that separates us from ourselves? This is the most important of all voyages of discovery, and without it, all the rest are not only useless, but disastrous.*
> —Thomas Merton

Everyone needs a place and a time where they can reconnect with themselves, and hopefully, either find or rediscover God in the process. What that looks like is as unique as the individual who practices this thing that many loosely describe as meditation. My own quiet contemplation takes place late at night when we have laid the day to rest for all practical purposes and nothing remains but for body and mind to relax. That is the time I retreat to the greenhouse, our garden room that has become sacred space within a larger context I call *Pa Amani*.[44] My own experience of regular reflection may best be termed modified meditation; whereas eastern meditation aims at emptying oneself, Christian meditation seeks a greater filling of oneself with the person of Jesus Christ, something that is far more active than it is passive. These are the times a relaxed body

---

[43] According to urbandictionary.com, *insomniatic* is "the state of mind where one becomes addicted to the deprivation of sleep caused by an epic revelation of joy."

[44] Swahili for "place of peace."

and focused mind seem to foster intense creativity. In other words, I am still, but not immobile. Granted I had the energy during late-night inspiration to channel creative urges into art, but I am content to find energy sufficient to record my thoughts on paper, or smart phone, or whatever is within reach at the moment. Deep thought for me always leads to an effort to record it. I encourage experimentation with modified meditation. Retreat to your own holy place and take with you something with which to record your thoughts. Think and write, or draw, or paint, and think some more. "Art enables us to find ourselves and lose ourselves at the same time."[45] Then share your results with others. Solitude was never intended as a selfish exercise. What you encounter may surprise you; you just may come upon yourself and find that behind it all is a loving Father beckoning you to embrace him by knowing and sharing yourself with someone else.

Why retreat from the noise? Why escape the constant parade of heightened decibels and vitriolic chatter that startles and shatters the serenity of the quiet heart? No possible reason exists apart from this—solitariness creates quiet space for deep reflection, meditation, contemplation. In other words, solitude allows one to think. Herein lies the problem—too many of us abhor thought. Activity and noise trump the quiet pursuit of contemplation. "The desperate need today is not for a greater number of intelligent people or gifted people, but for deep people."[46] Depth of personhood comes not from noise but from peace that makes sense out of both sound and soundlessness. If one creates space to think, he or she may indeed be startled at both the brutality and beauty of the discovery; however, those who are never introduced to themselves cannot be Christ's disciples. The rarity of ardent discipleship is directly connected to the scarcity of solitude.

†

---

[45] Thomas Merton, *No Man Is an Island* (Boston: Mariner Books, 2002).

[46] Richard Foster.

Thingamabob, doomahickey, whatchamacallit—these are just some of the words I use when at a loss for other more concrete ones. Advanced academic degrees notwithstanding, I am often stumped to describe the simplest of objects. That same dumbfoundedness is the common experience of all authentic worship. Much of what passes for religion these days is too easily explained; holy stuttering is in short supply in postmodernity. Very little mystery remains after singing choruses in rounds and learning five suggestions for upgrading one's life, making church more akin to Wall Street than the *Via Dolorosa*. "Worship" services (I confess I have never understood why they are termed *services*—who exactly is serving and being served anyway?) follow well-rehearsed schedules, such that if the Holy Spirit is to show up at all, he had better take care of business in an hour. Performance claims the prize, and somehow we have convinced ourselves that grand productions draw "seekers" to the Gospel like so many moths to the flame. Conventional wisdom would state flatly that if I am looking for slick entertainment, I will always find it somewhere other than church, regardless of how much is spent to convince otherwise.

Whatever happened to sacred mystery? When did we decide that we could package the Holy Other into bite-size portions, easily digested, and just as readily forgotten? When was the last time that a glimpse of the suffering Savior or conquering Christ seized the heart and would not let go? How long has it been since the Ground of all Being grabbed you and you could not speak or cry or move in response? If I am able to fully plan and explain worship, the object must be something other than the One "who is and who was and who is to come, the Almighty."[47] True worship elicits wonder, and wonder eventually gives way to transformation.

> *Silent night! Holy night!*
> *Shepherds quake at the sight!*
> *Glories stream from Heaven afar,*
> *Heavenly Hosts sing Alleluia!*

---

[47] Revelation 1:8 (NRSV).

ORDINARY GLORY

Christ, the Savior, is born!
Christ, the Savior, is born!

Shepherds quaked at the sight, and who could blame them? Sensitive sheepherders reacted as one might expect when confronted by a choir of angels. These men who struggled to eke out a hard scrabble life upon the cold and foreboding plains of Israel were among the first granted a wondrous revelation, and it sent them to their shaking knees. Is it wrong to admit physical reaction to spiritual reality? I hope not. From childhood church services at Trinity Baptist Church to Royal Ambassador campfires on the Easley's farm, from grand houses of worship in Britain to thatched huts in Kenya's northern frontier, I have trembled at the overwhelming nearness of the Almighty. A disturbing trend is afoot in contemporary Christianity bent on removing mystery from devotion; it may be easier to tame the wind than keep our hearts in check when overwhelmed by grace. Though modern sensibilities may resist, trembling depicts an essential movement of the heart before God. One needs look no farther than the Psalms to find individuals whose Godward reaction is both physical and audible. The Psalmists groan, cry, moan, laugh, long, desire, despise, dance, and shout; authentic and spontaneous, the Psalms disclose a sinner's honest response to the overwhelming majesty of God. If we would understand their songs and allow them to nurture our inner life, we too must learn to tremble before our Creator; sadly, the physical and emotional experience of awe is largely absent from what is smugly termed *worship* today. Desensitized by our own living, we are numb to the holy. Our pace of life and even the noise in church can drown out a thunderous divine voice. Joining the masses of popular culture that see at best a god who is distant and unlikely to be encountered in the "real world," many run aground on social sandbars, rejecting any sense of wonder having been persuaded that it simply isn't sophisticated to allow religion to touch them deeply or, heaven forbid, visibly.

Trembling is not our main concern, of course, but I hesitate to be at ease too quickly. It seems odd that while all creation shudders before the power and purity of the Exalted One, we should proceed routinely. From Belshazzar's knees clattering together, through the stirring Quaker and Puritan revivals, and on up to modern times, many have had a physical response to the reality of God. The mind, body, psyche, and spirit are woven together so tightly that we should expect to be affected as whole persons when we sincerely encounter God. Fearing God in the Psalms does not primarily mean quivering in anxiety and terror, but instead describes a profound sense of reverence. The Hebrew words most often used for "fear" in the Old Testament depict God as one who elicits ultimate respect. The heart of this experience is acknowledging the superiority of God over against ourselves. We are sullen and erratic, but God never gets the blues. For him to be moody would imply that he is better at one moment than he is at another, and that would be heresy. "Jesus Christ is the same yesterday and today and forever."[48] I wrestle regularly with a self-imposed inclination to gauge God's goodness or its opposite according to the unreliable emotion of the moment, as if his character fluctuates like the Dow Jones. God is wholly other, and encountering the Holy One leaves us awestruck. I am in constant danger of re-creating God according to my own image. A milquetoast deity frequently fits the bill. When it comes to the way God looks at me, I want Mr. Rogers, not William the Conqueror—soft when it comes to my shortcomings, understanding when it comes to my errors, and tender when it comes to my failure. The last thing I want is a standard bearer, a strong and demanding warrior captain, a relentless coach who will not settle for anything less than that for which I was created. I may be hard on myself, but God should take it easy on me. There is only one problem with this whole business—the omnipotent one refuses to fit into molds of my own making. Ours is a god of grace, but his mercy is juxtaposed to relentless expectation. We may respond with tears of praise or great waves of laughter and joy rolling out of every corner of our being, or open-mouthed astonishment may strike us silent. Christ the Savior is born, and it is incumbent upon us to bow in his presence.

---

[48] Hebrews 13:8 (NRSV).

ORDINARY GLORY

✝

No doubt you have heard the phrase "familiarity breeds contempt." While that may be true in some areas of life, I hesitate to apply it to biblical truth. Instead, presumption feeds apathy. Familiarity with the story of the cross may be the very thing that distances us from its impact. We become in the worst sense of the word, "objective." There is grave danger in studying theology with a mind divorced from the heart. We speak about things like incarnation, justification, atonement, redemption, sanctification, and do it all from the comfortable distance of third person. He did this. He said that. He is prophet, priest, and king. "*He.*" But God orchestrated human redemption so that we may move from third to first and second person—"I" and "You." "*I* once was lost but now am found." "*You* are Lord of heaven and earth." "*You* are *my* savior and *my* God." We may speak intelligently and convincingly of Jesus Christ and his earthly ministry, his compelling teaching and convincing miracles. We may wax eloquent concerning his courageous response to scourging and triumphant declaration from the cross, but what makes the whole thing matter is when I am able to say for myself:

> *Amazing grace, how sweet the sound*
> *That saved a wretch like me.*
> *I once was lost, but now am found,*
> *Was blind but now I see.*

Worship is much more alignment than activity. I worship best when my heart aligns with God's and the moment his interests begin to dictate my own. In this way worship consists largely of listening, granting space and thought to what the Father wants. Along the way, worship *becomes* my life, and every thought translates into divine dialogue. The awful hollowness of a day lived apart from conscious awareness of God's presence is excruciating enough to create an insatiable longing to be enveloped by him. King James English expresses it, "As the deer panteth for the water, so my soul longeth after Thee,

Oh God."[49] A more familiar modern declaration is, "Lord, I'm desperate for You." Both express recognition of a bankrupt heart bending and clinging to the hem of his garment. St. Bernard of Clairveaux states it well:

> *We taste Thee, O Thou Living Bread*
> *And long to feast upon Thee still:*
> *We drink of Thee, the Fountainhead*
> *And thirst our souls from Thee to fill.*[50]

Never relinquish poverty of spirit in favor of smug self-sufficiency.

†

Although no expert on the book of Revelation, I once preached a series of sermons on the seven messages given by Christ to seven historic churches in chapters 2 and 3 of the apocalypse. Near the end of his address to the church in Pergamum, there is a curious statement about Christ giving "hidden manna" to those believers who refuse compromise and persevere in their faith despite difficult times. I shared that my best take on this is that God assures us he is aware of and concerned about what we need. As I spoke, I looked into pairs of interested but hurting eyes, a few blank stares, and more than a few sets searching to see if I knew by experience what in heaven's name I was talking about.

One thing I have learned is to resist the tendency to define God by what I need. While "God is all I need" sounds pious, the truth is that God is far more than what I need and what you need and what the whole world ever has or ever will need. When I self-prescribe blinders so that all I see is my pain and judge God accordingly, I reduce him to a shadow of myself. Does God care? Absolutely! Is God the solution? Without a doubt. But the Creator and Sustainer

---

[49] Psalm 42:1 (KJV).
[50] Bernard of Clairveaux, *Jesus, Thou Joy of Loving Hearts*, translated from Latin to English by Ray Palmer, 1858, in his *Poetical Works* (New York, 1876).

cannot be contained by imagination or confined by despair. Instead of asking God to act the way I want at any given moment, I must bow before him, surrender unconditionally, then allow God to reveal his glory and plan in spite of my circumstance.

I am familiar with the way the Westminster Shorter Catechism begins: "The chief end of man is to glorify God and enjoy Him forever," and while I would never dispute that declaration, it halts short of depicting the fullest design of human existence. This thought struck home when concluding worship one evening. I prayed for each of us to serve moment by moment as reflections of grace because doing so adds a horizontal dimension to the vertical expressed in "glorifying God and enjoying him." Perhaps the most far-reaching way I glorify God is by reflecting his grace to others—grace received transmutes to grace extended. This is the clearest imitation of Christ. Nothing more profoundly honors God than acting like him in relation to all others. The more clearly we reflect grace, the more we resemble a god of mercy. As Saint Francis prayed:

> *Lord, make me an instrument of Your peace. Where there is hatred, let me sow love; where there is injury, pardon; where there is doubt, faith; where there is despair, hope; where there is darkness, light; where there is sadness, joy. O, Divine Master, grant that I may not so much seek to be consoled as to console; to be understood as to understand; to be loved as to love; For it is in giving that we receive; it is in pardoning that we are pardoned; it is in dying that we are born again to eternal life.*

Authentic worship transforms inside and out.

†

Lake Pontchartrain Causeway spans twenty-four miles from North Shore to New Orleans and is the longest bridge over water in the world. Driving over bridges makes me nervous (gross understatement—just ask my wife) because they typically rise high to allow ships to pass beneath, but I actually relish traversing this exaggerated viaduct because it lies flat above the lake's surface and affords expansive water views in all directions. On one morning's drive to Louis Armstrong New Orleans International Airport from Covington, a squadron of pelicans bobbed in syncopation atop the choppy surface to my right while terns took turns (pun intended) plunge-diving the surface in search of breakfast. Shimmering on the gossamer horizon to the south stood the stair-stepped skyline of the Crescent City. All of it was, in a word, beautiful. Perhaps due to being back in the city of my birth and subsequent adoption, or possibly the result of observing the rebuilding still underway a decade following Katrina's rage, but for reasons I cannot fully explain, that morning over Lake Pontchartrain, I detected a melody of mercy. Thank God I did not miss the moment or the message.

Worship is a way of life as well as theological truth. Grace for living is most clearly seen in those unrehearsed moments when life suddenly makes sense, snapshots in time that pass all too quickly but for an instant remind us that life is purposeful after all. I have not always excelled at recognizing or reveling in mercy. I endured a span of time in my forties in which, although I still struggled to walk with the Lord, I interpreted grace as a figment of ancient writers' imaginations, a cruel joke played on the unsuspecting and naive. Promises violated by those I previously trusted and dismembered dreams derailed my confidence in God and myself, handing down a harsh reminder that there is no plot without conflict and that stories do not always enjoy happy endings. During those dark days, God more resembled judge than father. I prayed out of ingrained duty, and my meager offerings recoiled across the emptiness of my own heart. Fortunately for all of us, brokenness lays the brickwork for awakening. Revival emerges from the wake of great loss, and grace is most clearly detected in the dark. Father reached deep down and pulled me surface-ward so that I could breathe again. It was then that I heard again the strain of mercy that hurt had muffled and all but extinguished. Grace is always present tense, which means God is author of infinite second chances; the challenge is to see for yourself and courageously follow mercy back to the heart of a loving father. We cannot hold moments forever; they touch us as they pass and draw our heart to the one who lives above and beneath them.

SIX

Surrender

Here is a rule for everyday life: Do not do anything you cannot offer to God.
—St. John Vianney

One of the things I like most about our country bungalow is the fireplace. What I like least is that it doesn't work. We moved into this house nine years ago, and I remember how I could hardly wait for the warmth and ambiance of a crackling fire in the den to ease the morning chill and create snuggle space for my wife and I. The morning after move-in, I was sipping my first cup of morning coffee when misplaced light caught my eye. If I stood just right, I could detect shafts of daylight finding their way between tired bricks from the outside in. Enthusiasm over anticipated moments near a warming hearth quickly cooled as we learned that the fireplace was structurally questionable. The decision was made to cap the chimney and seal the fireplace opening with a sheet of heavy plastic purchased from Home Depot for the purpose, a conclusion and corresponding action guided by both safety and economy. The bottom line is that this lowered our utility bill, but money in the bank does not create warm memories. Still longing for the mood and tone of a fire's warming glow if not from embers themselves, I stumbled upon fake fire in an antique store. The logs are authentic, but behind them is a lightbulb and electric spinning wheel that yields the illusion of fire. The wood is real, but the flames are not; it gives the impression of fire.

I plugged in my "fire," sat on the nearby couch, and watched the electric display while imagining crackling cedar, aroma of a memory I would never know. An uninvited thought came to me, more challenge than it was a question. Am I like imaginary fire? Do I craft a clever ruse, but when examined closely expose electrical cord and spinning wheel? Does the substance of me radiate authentic glow for others to warm themselves by, or do they walk away cold and empty wondering what real fire feels like? Saint Paul draws a similar conclusion when he says that without love he is nothing more than an impressive show with a disappointing punch line. It will cost me something, perhaps a great deal, but the time may be right for removing the plastic, dismantling the chimney cap, chinking bricks, repairing the flue, and coaxing the fireplace to yield what it was created for—heat from real flames. And surely the moment is right for refusing to hide behind subterfuge and masquerade so that I fulfill all I was created to be.

†

*God teaches the soul by pains and
obstacles, not by ideas.*
—Jean-Pierre de Caussade

Our daughter had friends from California staying with them for a few days, and one of them was a yoga instructor. She graciously offered to put us through the paces if interested, and four of us agreed. We lowered the living room lights, spread bath towels on the ceramic tile, and did our best to bend our bodies on command. At one point I looked down and couldn't determine how my leg had made its way in front of my hand while the other leg bent at an odd angle in the opposite direction. I felt like a pretzel, ready to take up Twister again after all these years. We completed thirty minutes of synchronized suffering and agreed to do it all over again the next day. Anxiety mounted when it became apparent early in the second session that our daughter's friend had taken it easy on us during the first. Convinced that we could handle it, she pushed past the dimension of discomfort and into the arena of pain. I kept asking myself why I had agreed to this torture, and decided that yoga is a four-letter word in more ways than one. When I lightheartedly commented on the misery of the exercise, the instructor smiled and pleasantly stated that expanded flexibility could add years to my life or, at the very least, would enhance the quality of whatever quantity I end up with. In the aftermath, I discovered that my back felt better than it had in a very long time. Momentary misery is evidently worth the long-term benefit.

Left to myself, I choose comfort over commitment every time, precisely the reason I cannot trust the decision to myself—I must live the crucified life so that the choice is always up to him. Dying today translates into life I never fathomed possible. Death to self does not mean emptiness; instead, crucifixion means spiritual altitude—life on a higher plane than I would have chosen for myself otherwise. In order to soar, we must first advance to abandonment. Rather than passive inactivity, the crucified life insists that we take action, cutting erroneous ties and re-lashing our moorings to Christ. Along with the Prodigal, "I will arise and go to my father."[51] I will wake up, get up, grow up, and climb up. I choose to discard the garbage piling up in heart and mind. Ruthlessly, I inventory motive and attitude and address each in desperate fashion. I recalibrate my attention to Christ with savage intentionality. "Reckon yourselves dead to sin." This is no valley of ease; this is a summit to scale under harrowing and hellish conditions. Crucifixion places me precariously on a rocky crag with no safety net below, and bids me ever higher.

†

Thirty-six years ago, my best friend and I embarked on an epic journey. Fresh out of high school and sporting my own set of wheels, I somehow convinced my friend's naïve parents to trust him into my care for a road trip from Port Arthur to Mississippi and back again. My ace in the hole was that our destination was a church camp and

---

[51] Luke 15:18 (KJV).

that the purpose of this extended soirée was spiritual growth. They consented, and we departed. Oh, the feeling of youthful independence, conquering asphalt in a rust-red tank officially identified as a 1965 Ford Galaxy, heating pork and beans for dinner at roadside parks, and singing off-key at the top of our lungs to music blasting from state-of-the-art 8-track.

Dark-thirty in some obscure-to-me portion of Mississippi, radio blaring to stay awake behind the wheel, we navigated a blind curve without noticing an unlighted railroad crossing warning. Neither of us saw the sign in the dark because we were too busy singing to pay attention, so we emerged from the bend just as a train approached the intersection from the west. The locomotive's horn roared, I stomped the accelerator, and somehow we crossed the tracks just ahead of the train, feeling its draft as we plunged past. Stunned into silence, I pulled the car to a stop on the side of the road to allow time to collect what remained of our nerves, and recount what just almost happened. As we debriefed, we were convinced that God had rescued us from ourselves and decided that it was as good a time as any to prepare to die. We hastily scribbled a note to the effect that if anyone found us dead, they were to rest assured that we knew the Lord and that we wished the same for them. To cap it all off, we lay awake long enough that night to commit to memory what has become my life verse—Galatians 2:20. For the first time in my life, I had a glimpse of the truth that no one is ready to live unless they've tasted death in themselves.

> *I am crucified with Christ: nevertheless, I live; yet not I, but Christ liveth in me: and the life which I now live in the flesh I live by the faith of the Son of God, who loved me, and gave himself for me.*[52]

I had no idea at that moment how important that lesson would prove to be.

---

[52]   Galatians 2:20 (KJV).

Fifteen years later, I was a newly appointed missionary to Kenya and fledgling student in the Kiswahili language school at Brackenhurst, which may seem an odd name for an African landmark. It was originally called Three Tree Farm because of three tall *Muna* trees that served as a landmark for wagons coming up from Nairobi. The Hudson Cane family emigrated there in 1914 from a place called Brackenhurst near Southall, Nottinghamshire County, England, to what was then British East Africa, and when they arrived and saw the bracken fern growing on the numerous hills (*hurst*), they changed its name to Brackenhurst. One Saturday morning, a fellow missionary student and I set out from language school high atop the tea fields of Tigoni and headed down to Nairobi for the pleasant task of refereeing basketball games at Rosslyn Academy. I was more along for the ride than anything else, although I was the one driving. Sports have long been a passion of mine, but I have managed generally to remain on the playing side of things rather than officiating, so when asked to help out, I reluctantly agreed, largely because life moves slowly in Africa and it seemed like a good way to spend the day. The games proved uneventful. I do not remember a great deal about the performance of the teams or my own on the court, but I recall clearly what happened on the drive back home.

The elevation gradually increases three thousand feet as one makes the climb from Nairobi northwest toward the next largest town of Limuru and its surrounding tea plantations. Under ordinary driving conditions, this would pose little or no problem, but we were traveling in a language student mission-issued Peugeot, which left a great deal to be desired under any circumstance. My missionary companion provided driving directions, having been in country longer than me, and because I remain inherently directionally challenged. He motioned for me to leave Limuru Road and turn onto Red Hill Road in order to save some time and enjoy the scenery since we were forced to crawl at a snail's pace anyway. Vehicles passed us with some regularity, so I wasn't paying much attention when a Toyota pickup pulled alongside us, fell behind, and then approached again. The second approach caused me to look more closely, and when I did, I saw a man pointing a gun from the truck window nearest me, motioning animatedly at me to pull over to the side of the road. I ignored him until the driver of the truck veered sharply left, forcing us off the road and to an abrupt stop. Five men unfolded from the cab of the small Toyota and surrounded our car. Our windows were rolled down due to the warmth of the day, so the men jabbed machine guns through the openings and up against our faces. The cold of the blue steel was shocking. My colleague whispered that we should refrain from looking directly at the bandits in hope they would leave us unharmed. I felt compelled to say something, but the only thing I had learned to say in Swahili to that brief point in my studies was the equivalent of "How are you today?" which seemed anything but appropriate, so I remained silent. The men speaking in broken English commanded us to give them our money and watches. Then they told us to leave our vehicle and begin walking. One of them said in a voice I will never forget, "Leave the car. Today you die."

    I had heard it said that at moments such as the one I was presently enduring, a person's life passed before their eyes. That may have been true for others, but all I could think of was what a terrible mess God had made of *my* life. I hastily hurled accusations at God for having coerced me into leaving the comfort of my home and relatively successful ministry in America, only to travel halfway around the world to die before leading any African to Christ or proclaiming the Gospel to anyone with an African tongue. God interrupted my mental tirade by evoking the memory of what I had learned that night fifteen years before near a darkened train track in rural Mississippi: "I am crucified with Christ." That was all it took to remind me that this life is no longer mine, and God can do whatever he pleases with it. The release of that moment's surrender was so profound that I did not notice the men climbing back into their truck. I snapped to attention when they gunned by us, and we watched spellbound as one man held something out the window of the truck and dropped it to the tarmac. When they veered out of sight, we went to retrieve what they had left and to our surprise learned that they had returned the keys to our car. Even bandits were not interested in a language school Peugeot. My friend and I drove slowly back to Brackenhurst, more out of shock than the demands of the steep grade. After we told our story to those interested enough to listen, I found a quiet place and settled down to think and pray. I exhaled with the obvious relief of surviving the ordeal, but more than anything else, from the realization that I had been relieved of the awful burden of needing to survive. Something within me had died, and something stronger had assumed its place. Disciples are dead men walking; we belong to Christ. As counterintuitive as it sounds, surrender is the gift we give ourselves. Christ may do with us what he wills, and we are always the better for it.

> *When Christ calls a man, He bids him come and die. It may be a death like that of the first disciples who had to leave home and work to follow Him, or it may be a death like Luther's, who had to leave the monastery and go out into the world. But it is the same death every time—death in Jesus Christ, the death of the old man at his call.*[53]

Some things in life are immune to personal preference. You may opt for oatmeal over Rice Chex, prefer blueberries to apples, or select rhubarb pie instead of mincemeat, and no one, including you will suffer for your choices. Others matter a great deal more. You really have no say in whether or not your heart pumps blood on autopilot throughout your limbs, or if touching a hot stove top will burn and blister your skin. Local ordinance demands that there be negative consequences for ignoring a burn ban and setting fire to the expanding mountain of brush behind my house. I might prefer to speak on my cell phone in a school zone, but that was never a good idea and no longer an option in this country. The same is true with both the horizontal and vertical aspects of discipleship. Grace is never neutral. Nothing needs to change in order to experience God's grace, but once we do, everything must radically change—more out of divine necessity than individual choice. Grace does not demand that we

---

[53] Dietrich Bonhoeffer, *The Cost of Discipleship* (New York: Touchstone, 1995).

clean up our act; it mandates a funeral pyre—death to self and all that accompanies our egocentric lifestyle. Surrender isn't surrender if I ferret away something in reserve.

✝

> *A vision of God secures humility. Seeing God for who He is enables us to see ourselves for what we are. This makes us bold, for we see clearly what great good and evil are at issue, and we see that it is not up to us to accomplish it, but up to God—who is more than able. We are delivered from pretending, from being presumptuous about ourselves, and from pushing as if the outcome depended on us. We persist without frustration, and we practice calm and joyful noncompliance with evil of every kind.*
> —Dallas Willard

A legend from India tells of a mouse who was terrified of cats until a magician agreed to cast a spell and transform him into a cat. That resolved his fear until he met a dog, so the magician turned him into one. The "mouse turned cat turned dog" was content until he met a tiger, so once again the magician turned him into what he feared. But when the "mouse turned cat turned dog turned tiger" came to the magician complaining that he had met a hunter, the magician refused to help. "I will make you into a mouse again, for though you have the body of a tiger, you still have the heart of a mouse." Attitude is everything.

Once, Winston Churchill was sitting on a platform waiting to speak to a large crowd that had gathered to hear him. The chairman of the event leaned over and said, "Isn't it exciting, Mr. Churchill, that all these people came to hear you speak?" Churchill responded, "It is quite flattering, but whenever I feel this way I always remember that if, instead of making a political speech I was being hanged, the crowd would be twice as big." While poverty of character is never encouraged, Jesus himself raises the right estimation of oneself to the highest possible priority. *Blessed are the poor in spirit: for theirs is the kingdom of heaven.*[54] Only when I see myself in light of Christ and evaluate myself accordingly am I able to embrace the heart of God rather than that of a mouse.

A great chasm yawns between disciplined believers and spiritual couch potatoes. Grace was never intended to produce flabby Christians. Although we rightfully gorge ourselves on an all-you-can-eat smorgasbord of mercy, Scripture expects the opposite of spiritual obesity—out-of-shape believers lumbering lethargically through their spiritual journey. Grace results in heightened passion to pursue God, or we misunderstand its divine intent; grace and hunger are not only compatible, they are conjoined at the heart. The Bible unapologetically urges those who are being saved to strive, and those who have been found by grace to stay after the search for greater intimacy with the grace giver. Perhaps the best known story of pursuit in all of American literature is Herman Melville's 1851 epic tale of Captain Ahab and a giant white sperm whale. Ishmael narrates the voyage of the whaler *Pequod* and its captain's crazed pursuit of Moby Dick, which on a previous voyage destroyed Ahab's ship and severed his leg below the knee. Unlike Ahab in his maniacal pursuit for revenge in the shadow of enormous loss, each of us is to be engaged in an all-consuming high and noble quest in light of inexplicable gain.

In what should be required reading for every believer, Tozer writes:

> *The yearning to know what cannot be known, to comprehend the incomprehensible, to touch and taste the unapproachable, arises from the image of God in the nature of man. Deep calleth unto deep, and though polluted and landlocked by the mighty*

---

[54] Matthew 5:3 (KJV).

disaster theologians call the Fall, the soul senses its origin and longs to return to its source.[55]

This insatiable appetite for personal intimacy with Almighty God is the antidote for what Bonhoeffer terms *cheap grace*. "Cheap grace is the grace we bestow on ourselves. Cheap grace is the preaching of forgiveness without requiring repentance, baptism without church discipline, Communion without confession . . . Cheap grace is grace without discipleship, grace without the cross, grace without Jesus Christ, living and incarnate."[56] Grace pardons completely, and authentic discipleship accepts with it greater opportunity and responsibility, rather than entitlement.

†

I sat on a love seat in a small bedroom on the third floor of Sweet Cane Inn in Natchitoches, Louisiana, sipping a cup of Community Coffee and looking out a window that is original to this house constructed for Congressman Phanor Breazeale in the late 1800s. My vantage point allowed a view of certain treetops near the Cane River, but I was as much intrigued by the tall, narrow window as I was the view it afforded. Vintage glass appeals to me; unquestionably imperfect, but its very imperfection is what piques my interest. Images seen through vintage glass appear slightly distorted due to the ripple effect of the glaze itself. The aged glass adds texture to the light that filters through it and becomes a thing of beauty all its own, without distracting from the image on the other side.

I cannot help but see this as a great commentary on the properly viewed and powerfully lived Christian existence. Our calling is to allow Christ to show through us, but the inescapable reality is that anything passing through us will be either slightly or greatly distorted

---

[55] A. W. Tozer, *The Pursuit of God* (Michigan: Bethany House, 2013).

[56] Dietrich Bonhoeffer, *The Cost of Discipleship* (New York: Touchstone, 1995).

by us. That need not be completely negative, if indeed it is negative at all. God intends to use flawed human beings in showing himself to the world. Just like vintage glass, we add texture to the light that passes through us. We may distort his image slightly, but Christ must sound and look something like us in order for people to understand him at all. Without us as a filter, God remains an abstract thought, a truth to which we give assent but never know. Jesus speaks of this in his parable of the vine that we read about in John 15. He is the grapevine and we are the branches, and the only way the world will comprehend the value of the vine is by seeing and tasting the fruit that the branches produce.

> *Turn around and believe that the good news that we are loved is better than we ever dared hope, and that to believe in that good news, to live out of it and toward it, to be in love with that good news, is of all glad things in this world the gladdest thing of all. Amen, and come Lord Jesus.*[57]

Nothing produces more fruit than compelling love. The finest example of this simple obsession that I have witnessed personally is Phillip Ingida D'ima. When I met him many years ago in the Kaisut Desert, he was stumbling from hut to hut in Kenya's northern frontier district, sharing the message of Christ's liberating love among the largely unreached Borana of Olla D'aba, a village near the isolated town of Marsabit. Philip walks with a limp because of a leg deformed by childhood polio. I will never forget Phillip's response when asked one day why he pushed through enormous pain so that he could declare his testimony of God's grace. He said simply, "Because I love Jesus. What other reason is there?"

†

---

[57] Frederick Buechner.

DANE FOWLKES

According to most philosophers, God in making the world enslaved it. According to Christianity, in making it, He set it free. God had written, not so much a poem, but rather a play; a play he had planned as perfect, but which had necessarily been left to human actors and stage-managers, who had since made a great mess of it.
—G. K. Chesterton, *Orthodoxy*

    I am not a traveling salesman, but my vocation lends itself to a goodly measure of mobility. My most recent journey included the small West Texas town of Anson in Jones County. Having spent my childhood on the Gulf Coast, driving through the vast expanse of West Texas feels like journeying to a foreign land, stepping back through time, returning to my travels across the Kaisut Desert of northern Kenya. Dust regularly rises and settles, turning back on itself like flour vapors migrating this way and that as chef tosses and flattens pizza dough into the desired consistency. I once saw so many towering dust devils on the lonesome stretch from Pecos to Fort Davis that I lost count of them. At times it seems like one drives great distances simply to go from one furnace blast to the next. Approaching Anson, the parched landscape gradually gave way to a smattering of paved streets and correspondingly few mottled buildings situated around an aged courthouse. The town, originally called Jones City, was built in anticipation of the arrival of the Texas and Pacific Railroad. Investments were made and stores and hotels opened, but the railroad went farther south. Jones City was declared the county seat in 1881, but the name was changed to Anson in 1882 without much opposition since Anson and Jones were the same man. A physician, San Jacinto veteran, publisher, founding member of the first Masonic Lodge in Texas, Jones was president of the Republic of Texas and Texas's ambassador to the United States. He is buried in Houston, and there is no record of him ever traveling near the county that bears his name.

    I arrived forty-five minutes early for my appointment, so I crisscrossed the small town, more or less to kill time. I came across a couple of secondhand shops that looked like they contained third- or fourth-hand items, a post office, two churches, a Dollar General store, and a weathered billboard advertising the Cowboy Christmas Ball at Anson's historic Pioneer Hall, but the images that held my attention comprised a large set of murals on the south side of one of the buildings southwest of the Courthouse Square. Large painted letters below the murals indicated that they were provided by a grant from a foundation in Wichita Falls. I sat and studied through my driver's side window what promised to one day be an incredible array of paintings. Each separate section contained distinct figures depicting the history of cotton industry in the area. While the outlines were distinct, there was very little color on the whitewashed wall, only a pale patch here and there. Glancing at my watch, I saw that it was time to move to my meeting, and I decided to ask the man I had come to see about the status of the paintings. I navigated the one-way streets to the east side of the square, parked, and walked inside. I shook hands with my new acquaintance and accepted his offer to sit near his desk. We engaged in the usual small talk between strangers meeting for the first time, which included references to weather and current events. Somewhat in passing, I mentioned the murals-in-process and stated that I hoped to return to see the finished product. My host smiled and told me that what I had seen actually was the finished product. He explained that the outdoor paintings were completed a decade earlier, but unlike the well-preserved post office mural "Cowboy Dance," the exposed pigments had fallen victim to the West Texas sun, and what I saw was the faded remainder of the vanishing artistic depiction of Jones County history. Other murals in Anson were in much better condition, one paying homage to cattle brands and another to Dr. Pepper. While I had initially thought the murals held promise, they would soon be nothing but a footnote to a small town's memory.

It is important to know whether you are coming or going. In a way that is hard to describe, the faded murals remind me of testimonies I've heard through the years. Testimony time in church has always been curious to me. Irrespective of age, one adult after another would share her or his faith story by recounting what had happened long before, at times including details as to the date and time they encountered the Savior. Each narrative was unique, the one common element being a distinct encounter in the distant past. I listened carefully, at times spellbound, only to wonder later what difference the historical event was making in the testifier's present and what impact it might have on his future. There is no such thing as standing still with one's relationship to Christ. We are either going or coming, growing or declining; at times, it is difficult to detect which way we're facing. The hallmark of Christian experience is a growing faith.

> *But grow in the grace and knowledge of our Lord and Savior Jesus Christ. To Him be the glory, both now and to the day of eternity. Amen.*[58]

> *Therefore, leaving the elementary teaching about the Christ, let us press on to maturity, not laying again a foundation of repentance from dead works and of faith toward God.*[59]

When you stop growing, you start dying. At any given moment in time, I am either a masterpiece in process or a fading image of what I once was, the ghost of what I was intended to be. The choice is mine.

†

It was providential that my first journey abroad for Samaritan's Purse took me through South Korea. I say that because my journey in missions began there thirty-six years ago. I arrived in 1979 for my second trip to Korea, that time to preach for the Jeil Baptist Church in Kwang Ju. I was nineteen years old and had sensed divine direction to preach from the time I was sixteen. I had gone to Korea two years earlier with a group from my church, but this time I was on

---

[58] 2 Peter 3:18 (NIV).
[59] Hebrews 6:1 (NIV).

my own, save for an aged chaperon affectionately known as Momma Tipps. She was a legendary missionary figure in our circles, having traveled innumerable times to San Andres Island in the Caribbean to share the gospel, almost singlehandedly reorienting Trinity Baptist Church toward the world. Momma Tipps and I traveled through Los Angeles, toured Hollywood, made the walk of stars in front of Grauman's Chinese Theatre, and then landed in Kwang Ju, South Korea. We spent nearly two weeks together. I'm not sure what she thought about me, but my awe of her grew exponentially.

Our last Sunday afternoon in Kwang Ju, we were invited to join missionaries from various Christian denominations for the missionary worship service held in Bell Chapel on the mountainside in rural Kwang Ju. In certain respects, this was just one more worship gathering; in other ways, it was extraordinary. God spoke, at least I understood him say that *this* was his calling for me, *this* meaning cross-cultural ministry. I returned to the United States determined to serve Christ as a foreign missionary. My path since then has taken me through a decade of service in Africa and India, dissolution of marriage, losing everything only to gain far more in return, and a new opportunity to fulfill God's call to missions. *This* looks differently today than it did all those years ago, but is no less fulfilling. God never forgets his call, even when we lose sight of it or make choices that obscure it. Grace is more than a means to salvation; grace is a way of life.

As a younger man, I convinced myself that I could change the world; now my greatest struggle is against the world changing me. Early on, my oil-refinery-worker father and church-librarian mother convinced me that I could do anything God placed on my heart to attempt. They provided a safe place and secure environment from which to dare and dream outrageous things. When I wanted to go with the World Evangelism Foundation to South Korea at age seventeen and again at age nineteen, they encouraged me and did what they could to help. My choice to attend East Texas Baptist University in order to prepare for Christian missions rather than accept scholarship offers elsewhere or pursuing a possible appointment to West Point did not lead them to believe I'd been abducted by aliens and brainwashed into servitude. As a pastor in East Texas, then Houston, and later as a missionary candidate, Mother remained my biggest fan and quietly encouraged me to follow God largely. She was schooled by listening to Robert Schuller preach his possibility message while keeping her spiritual feet planted firmly grounded through Oswald Chambers's teaching on the crucified life, and she championed my own pursuit of surrender. When I stayed the course to leave for Africa just four months after my father's death, Mom never complained or asked me to reconsider. My missionary service was always more of a sacrifice for her than it was for me.

Life is for me, in many ways, easier now than it has ever been. The challenge is to embrace crucified service in the midst of relative ease and comfort. I neither wear hardship as a badge of God's approval nor pray to be uncomfortable; I do petition the Father to stoke the embers of passionate devotion so that comfort never becomes my standard for appraising God's grace. If I have learned anything through the years, it is that abundant living is in no way connected to abundance, but is, instead, inseparable from surrender.

SEVEN

Family

> *When a man leaves home, he leaves behind some scrap of his heart. Is it not so, Godric?... It's the same with a place a man is going to. Only then he sends a scrap of his heart ahead.*
> —Frederick Buechner

How do you find your way home again? It is easier if you ever had a home to begin with. As a boy growing up in Port Arthur, home meant private time in my own bedroom, family gatherings around the kitchen table (with the exception of Dad who ate in his recliner with plate balanced on belly and paper napkin tucked under his chin), the independence of riding my bicycle to school, summers playing in Groves American Little League, and, much later, sitting in our high school football stadium stands awaiting my turn to walk across the makeshift stage and bring closure to the previous twelve years of public education. Home was my first hand-me-down car—a faded pink 1965 Rambler Classic, my first date, first job, my first anything and anywhere. One dictionary defines *home* as a place where something flourishes, is most typically found, or from which it originates. In a very real way, home is whatever convinces that you belong. People are the best at doing that—mother, father, sister, best buddy, favorite teacher, childhood nemesis, pastor, coach, next-door neighbor—a human mosaic that sounds, looks, and feels like home.

What's really odd is that the young spend their time trying to leave home while the old occupy their twilight years trying to find their way back. My favorite song as a teenager was the Merle Haggard classic "Ramblin' Fever," but my preferred tune these days is "There's No Place Like Home." What we're all searching for is a center, a fulcrum on which to fix our equilibrium, but we do not know this. We try to match the emotional attachments of our childhood with things that were never meant to satisfy our God-given longing. It is good theology to insert here that Christ is our center, but that doesn't tell the whole story. Magnetic north is something you cannot see; instead, what you observe is the needle that points that direction. In a similar way, home is our earthly needle—a person or persons that help orientate us toward the center. That explains why familial conflict is so destructive—we lose our bearings because we lose the very thing God intended to point us toward him. Some never find it again. Some think they do only to discover that what they thought was home is in reality a place where they do not belong or an experience that savagely disappoints. Blessed is the man or woman who experiences the grace of loving and being loved by someone who urges them back to center. Thomas Wolfe was wrong; you can go home again. When you find your way back, you will discover that home is a person pointing you still further back to Christ.

†

*How we spend our days is, of course,
how we spend our lives.*
—Annie Dillard

Christmas evokes powerful memories. Enjoying a blueberry bagel and orange juice for breakfast while sitting near the lighted Christmas tree in our den made me feel like a kid again. For some reason that I cannot adequately explain, I was small and young and innocent again, even though I'm actually slightly overweight, old, and saddle worn. For those few moments, I could see my father sipping morning Maryland Club and hear Mom baking biscuits from scratch behind him. Sister stood nearby holding kitchen towels that she insisted we place around our heads while reenacting the

Christmas story. At least she let me play Joseph; I prefer to forget the other times when she made me wear something much less masculine. A flash of light pulled my gaze to brightly papered packages encircling an artificial blue spruce like the Polar Express. Several items remained unwrapped —Santa's handiwork. The world was wonderful and small and uncomplicated then; love flowed freely and abundantly, and security had a face—two faces to be exact. Mom and Dad would always be there, and they still are after a fashion. There were no bills to pay and no battles to fight except the occasional one against my sister, especially when forced to share the rear bench seat of our '65 Rambler Classic on family vacation. Christmas was magical in my childhood, and I carry the miracle with me all these years later. The power of Christmas comes from the love we have for one another and the birth narrative we hold in common. When we exchange gifts, drink eggnog, sing carols, light candles, and relish the Christmas story, we are banking memories and extending the miracle for another generation.

> *When tradition is thought to state the way things really are, it becomes the director and judge of our lives; we are, in effect, imprisoned by it. On the other hand, tradition can be understood as a pointer to that which is beyond tradition: the sacred. Then it functions not as a prison but as a lens.*[60]

I have never been crazy about the day after; Christmas arrives and departs far too quickly. It feels like only yesterday that I was lugging our artificial tree in a wheelbarrow from barn to den and lowering unending boxes of ornaments down from the attic. Now the pressure is on to dismantle the Christmas tree and neatly stow away decorations for another year. Doing my best to stave off putting away Christmas is not another anemic delay. While I have not been without moments of procrastination (to put it mildly), this is not one of those unnecessary postponements. The prolonging of Christmas

---

[60] Marcus Borg.

wrap-up has nothing to do with laziness, and everything to do with reluctance.

My reticence to put away Christmas is complicated. I love Christmas and everything that goes along with it, and the joy I share with wife and family in preparing for Christmas and celebrating the days before the Christ-mass is exhilarating. Something about a lighted Christmas tree surrounded by a mosaic of packages in assorted shapes, sizes, and density glowing in the corner of the den until bedtime stirs me down deep inside. Tradition is tantamount to celebration. My wife and I enjoy simple ones like watching and listening to Bing Crosby while he croons "I'm Dreaming of a White Christmas" and portrays our favorite Irish priest of all time, Father O'Malley, in *Going My Way* and *Bells of St. Mary's*, gathering with family on Christmas Eve, and attending together the community candlelight and communion service. Like it or not, today's Christmas cheer turns into tomorrow's Christmas memory.

Each year's reluctance to close out the season comes more from a deep awareness of the brevity of life than from fascination with the sacred day. The absence of loved ones alters the tone and volume of celebration. Change is hard, especially when it means someone is missing. I still remember the third Christmas without Mom that was also our first without Popi, and much of each year's yuletide conversation takes the shape of memories of past Christmases enjoyed with them. They are not the only ones noticeably absent. Mr. Evans from down the lane has left us following a brief stint in a home for those who can't remember. Our neighbors' father is in a home for those who can remember, but have lost the physical strength to do much more than that. The absence of these I care about leads me to engage in soul searching of my own, and forces me to face squarely the fact that I have already celebrated more Christmases than I have left to celebrate—a sobering realization. Instead of mourning loss, I pay tribute to what has been before and extol the virtue of what remains. Everyone chooses her or his own memories. I have no option as to putting away Christmas for another year, but I choose to guard the memories and look for that which is holy in every day.

ORDINARY GLORY

✝

The grace of God means something like: Here is your life. You might never have been, but you are because the party wouldn't have been complete without you. Here is the world. Beautiful and terrible things will happen. Don't be afraid. I am with you. Nothing can ever separate us. It's for you I created the universe. I love you.
—Frederick Buechner

As far back as I can remember, I have felt special, due in no part to anything about me; instead, that impression has everything to do with my mother and father. My earliest memory goes something like this, "Son, you're special because we chose you." I did not comprehend it at the time, and they may not have fully understood it themselves, but Henry and Lois established a sure foundation from which to embrace the reality. Being adopted was better, in my undeveloped mind, than having been their natural-born son, although I secretly wished that I had inherited my father's height, his James Dean good looks, and his deep bass voice. Chalk it up to masterful child psychology coming from a boilermaker and a church librarian, mainly because it was heartfelt and honest. They were unable to have children of their own, so they chose to lavish their love on someone else's miscalculation, redeeming both child and themselves in the process. They believed adoption to be the will of God for them, and truth be known, it was for my sister and me as well.

I wish that every child could develop according to the strong impression that she or he is special and chosen for greatness. The truth is, life is special and you are too. The Father says to each of us, "You are special, because I chose you."

✝

DANE FOWLKES

I would give so much to know about who they were, both for its own sake and also for the sake of learning something more about who I am myself.
—Frederick Buechner[61]

Occasionally I wonder what it would have been like to have had a grandfather. Oh, I had grandfathers to be sure, only I never had the privilege of meeting any of them. To be completely open about it, I'll never know exactly how many I never knew. The ones I heard a smattering of stories about include James Nash Richey, an Irish barber who died in a Model T Ford on the way back to Port Neches from a hunting trip when his daughter, my mother, was still an infant. Mom was the youngest of six siblings, the four oldest being boys much older than she, and one older sister who was never fully there and later took her own life. All that remains of Grandpa Richey (I have no idea what moniker he would have chosen for himself) is a small, slightly faded black and white photograph that shows him standing behind an old-fashioned barber's chair with a customer seated near a counter littered about with glass bottles of lotion and talcum powder, brushes of various sizes and types, and a straight razor. Another bearded man stands in the corner of the image, and the whole scene leaves me wondering how long it was taken before the fatal Tin Lizzie accident, if these men were friends and perhaps hunting companions, why he chose barbering as his profession, whether or not he preferred sweet potato to pecan pie, and the like.

The other man who qualifies as my grandfather was Henry Pleasant Fowlkes. According to my mother (Dad never said much to me about his father), Grandpa Fowlkes was a kind and soft-spoken man driven to the drink by a not-so-kind and anything but soft-spoken wife. Evidently, Mamie Fowlkes made life a nightmarish version of hell on earth, and Henry did what he could to cope, drifting from job to job, selling used cars, delivering milk, working on assembly lines, and who knows what else. He came from good stock in Franklin,

---

[61] Frederick Buechner, *The Longing for Home: Recollections and Reflections* (San Francisco: Harper San Francisco, 1995).

Tennessee, and must have been something of a disappointment to his father, Henry Pleasant Sr., a Princeton alumnus who held prominent positions in Franklin as an attorney, judge, elder in the Presbyterian Church, Speaker of the House for the Tennessee legislature in 1879, and trustee of Central Hospital for the Insane for twenty years. Mom said that Dad's dad was generous to a fault, and died much too soon in her opinion, but perhaps just about right in his.

I have other grandfathers whose names I'll never know because of my dual heritage as an adopted son. Through genealogical research, I have learned something about my adoptive lineage, but only with an active imagination am I able to conjure up anything about my genetically connected heritage. I fantasized as a child, at times, about the circumstances that led a young woman to enter Sellers Baptist Home in New Orleans and then give birth to and relinquish her infant son, likely without ever knowing he had his father's blue eyes, or his grandfather's Romanesque nose, or his mother's lack of height with a propensity toward added weight showing up under his chin. She may have been a wealthy heiress attempting to protect her family from the disgrace of an illegitimate heir. Perhaps she was an exotic nightclub singer whose past caught up with her, or possibly a mysterious immigrant with nowhere else to turn. More likely, she was simply a naive young lady who made an inescapable blunder and opted to give away her mistake rather than attempt to erase it. What did her father think about her choices and actions? And then there's the "father." Did he know? Did he agree? Did he care? Did his father know? What did he think? What would he have thought about me?

There was one man who I asked to be my grandfather even though he wasn't. Henry Sutherland was a smallish, quiet man who was a member of our church in Port Arthur. I do not remember a lot about him except that he was a kindly henpecked man, and that he took care of the electronics related to our church's sound system, meaning he was always at church. One evening, the Sutherlands were visiting in our home, and I marched right up to him and asked him to be my grandfather. For years I called him Grandpa, and I think it made him feel special; we enjoyed an unusual bond, but I must admit that I allowed youth and distance to weaken its hold over time until it faded into the background without disappearing altogether.

What I do know is that I am who I am by the grace of God, and I am becoming who I will be because of that same grace. I did not choose the circumstances surrounding my origin any more than I could have worked my way into God's good graces; everything is according to the goodness and good pleasure of the Father. When I stop to notice my mirrored reflection, I have no clue who I might resemble, if, in fact, I resemble anyone at all. Grace is the looking glass that allows me to peer at myself and see what I can be, not what I once was.

†

It is funny how we loathe routine only to long for its return. Vacation is something we all anticipated intensely and greeted like the African Savannah welcomes the rains after a long dry season, but a break from normal demands is not always what we plan it to be. None of us would have imagined that we would spend our second day of vacation in a Nashville emergency room determining the seriousness of Joshua's abdominal pains. Even though we rejoiced that all tests for appendicitis or abdominal blockage were negative, we could not have predicted the physical and emotional toll the ordeal would take on us, and how it would temper each foray into the pool, time in the minivan, or any other vacation activity. There is no blame to be placed or shared; Josh's discomfort was simply a key theme in our story over the week of vacation.

Home is a word like *Mom*. It generally conjures up the warmest of feelings and the best of memories, but is rather hard to define. Is it a place or an experience, multiple places or a series of experiences? Josh set me to thinking about home because he said more than once that he wanted to go home, only one time he meant back to Waco and another time he was referring to our vacation cabin. While reflecting on the enigma, I read something from a former missionary colleague who has moved to Uganda after living and serving in Kenya more than twenty-five years. He writes, "Home! That sounds a bit strange to begin calling Kampala 'home', but it is." He goes on to mention his nervousness over learning a new city and language. For my missionary friend, home is obviously connected to both place and experience.

Later that same day, we toured the Battlefield of Spotsylvania Courthouse, sight of one of the bloodiest battles of the Civil War. Seventeen thousand men lost their lives in one day in the valley known as the Bloody Angle. As I walked the path of Lee's line, read the monuments, and touched the canons, I could not help but think that every blue-clad or gray-uniformed soldier who fought in that spot one hundred and fifty years before was likely filled with terror and a longing to go home. For some, home was magnetic north, for others it was magnetic south. But for all of them, home provided a bearing, a sense of knowing that no matter where they stood, they were either headed toward or away from home. Home is the place we were first and best loved, and we spend the rest of our lives trying to hold on or return to it. Blessed is the man or woman who finds it and recognizes it when they do.

Vacation is a lot like people-watching in an airport terminal, only you get to converse with some of them. We met an art gallery owner / English antique dealer in Gordonsville. He spoke with a distinct British accent, so I asked where he was from originally and learned that he hailed from Darby, England. The topic of conversation shifted to soccer when I asked if he was a "footballer," and he proceeded to wax eloquently about his days playing in the British 2nd level and later refereeing. He was particularly proud of the fact that the last match he officiated was Leicester versus Arsenal. Who would have expected to meet an English soccer player in Gordonsville, Virginia? We also met Sam from East Hanover County. He was the wrangler for our wagon ride at the resort, handling a team of white dappled Percherons named Doc and Duke. Sam is definitely down-to-earth; one might call him a man of the earth. He told us that he had been a teacher years ago and then was a dairy farmer for thirty years, doing all the work himself after his father died. He sold his cows back in 2007 just before the bottom dropped out of the market, but confided in us that he's still paying off what he lost when he sold. We encountered other interesting people, like the BBQ Exchange waitress stuck in the 1960s, complete with peace-sign-laden headband and long braided hair, and they remind me that each of us has a story and that our stories are unique. Jesus dealt with differences in a significant way—he met everyone where they were, spoke a language they understood, and always started with their particular context when sharing his message with them. The good news (Gospel) is a narrative of grace, custom fit for every individual.

When we had packed all we could into our allotted days, the cabin was cleaned, luggage stowed, snacks strategically placed, family members situated as comfortably as possible in their respective minivan locations, and all hunkered down for the nineteen-and-a-half-hour drive from Gordonsville, Virginia, to Waco, Texas. The most interesting thing to me about the whole experience was the question that both grandsons as well the adults voiced during our marathon journey back to Waco: where are we going next year? How can one long to return home and to leave it again, all in the same emotion? Familiarity breeds something far different from contempt; it provides a secure base from which to explore. Some of my happiest childhood memories are of the annual adventures our family took to Hot Springs, Arkansas. So strong are these sensory remembrances that they allow me to ignore anything negative, like the frequent spats with my sister over backseat territory, or my father's reluctance to stop along the drive for restroom breaks, or the way my parents had to carefully balance each travel expense with the more pressing demands of mortgage, car payment, and the like. Vacations were commas for Mom and Dad, but exclamation points for me and my sister, ones I'm grateful that I did not miss.

Jesus said, "The Father knows what we need."[62] He knows we need seasons, a measure of predictability that allows us space to create and courage to dare. He also knows that life without dreams leads to monotony, the shadow side of routine. So we struggle with an inherent tension—to remain and to release, to stay and to go, to be satisfied and to strain for something more, reminding us that we

---

[62] Matthew 6:8 (KJV).

were created for a relationship that may be enjoyed here and now, but that cannot be fully realized in this life. Missionary author Don Richardson called this "eternity in our hearts." Vacations are powerful experiences, simply because they remind our hearts that one day earthly and emotional seasons will be discarded in favor of uninterrupted perfection with the Father. In the meantime, we're thinking about crowding back into a minivan next summer and vacationing in Savannah.

†

Everyone needs a moment to put work on hold, abandon the mobile, and stealth away for space and peace. I'm not sure how you *carpe diem*, but my wife and I have found that we do it best by adding miles to my Jeep (affectionately nicknamed Ruby by our grandchildren) and transporting ourselves into an altered state that feels like vacation, even if it's just a day trek down the blacktop. The best part of traveling with my wife is that she reads aloud while I drive. Although she insists that it is simply to enrich us, I know she started doing it to keep me awake. Actually, the practice accomplishes both purposes. While keeping me alert behind the wheel, she has read to us novels and biographies, autobiographies and sermons. We've made friends in literature from slaves on antebellum Cane River plantations to an Episcopal priest in a small town named Mitford. One recent Sunday afternoon's drive began according to script, the second installment of a political autobiography that my wife started on our last adventure, but the return leg later in the evening contained a twist. As I drove (wide-awake I might add), something moved my soul, and I burst into a poor rendition of a favorite song from my teenage years, "Ramblin' Fever." My wife was startled, partly because it was off-key, but mainly because it was more than slightly out of character. What ensued were a couple of hours of something reminiscent of "Name That Tune." We sang the John Denver hits that had shaped my youth. We laughed through the best of the Beach Boys, including one tune I sing often to our grandchildren: "Oh, I'm long tall Texan, I ride a big white horse." Kenny Rogers made our memory hit parade, along with George Jones, Dolly Parton, and others. You could write a person's biography with the lyrics they memorize through the years. The most telling part of the experience was what we revealed and learned about each other, and what we remembered about ourselves. Having loved and lived with each other as best friends for a number of years, there is still so much to explore. The whole experience reminded me that all of us are works in progress. We may reach mile markers and achieve certain milestones, but none of us have fully arrived or ever will. Perhaps that's the point of humanity after all. To be fully human is to be in process; sometimes straining forward, other times pausing, but all the time growing.

†

It was an odd Fourth of July for our family because it was our first without Popi. He had not been with us for our family celebration the past two years due to deteriorating health, but even then, we took the party to him. The first such effort he seemed to recognize and appreciate, while the second escaped his largely expressionless stare. Alzheimer's is rarely forgiving, especially on holidays. The change was noticeable, yet he was still present in a way. In the past, Popi held center stage with his love for the great-grandchildren, for food, and for our annual *bocce* tournament. More than anything else, he simply loved the family being together. When the center is removed, what revolved around it tends to wobble while seeking a new focal point. When this happens, the whole thing appears out of sync, even slightly warped, like an old wooden tennis racket exposed to the elements. We pressed on and even persisted with the *bocce* tournament, naming it the Ury Armand Memorial Tournament, but we were conscious of the trying, which carries with it an emotional strain all its own. The good news is that wobbling objects often right themselves, and, no doubt, so will our family. We will once again celebrate in rhythm with one another and become unaware of what makes being family work. Thank God for making families resilient and for bestowing the gift of joy in spite of loss. "Sharing tales of those we've lost is how we keep from really losing them."[63] Popi is remembered, and remembering keeps him with us.

---

[63] Mitch Albom, *For One More Day* (New York: Hyperion, 2006).

ORDINARY GLORY

†

For a time, he was a soldier. With wiry frame and James Dean good looks, he walked first into the heart of Lois Richey and then rode onto the battlefield of Korea. An iron tank was his chosen coat of arms, and he commanded well just south of the DMZ. Occasionally, he weathered enemy fire while dishing out plenty of his own. Comrades in the Fourth armored division called him Hank; his bride called him sweetheart, and years later my sister and I called him Dad. His is one story among many, of men and women who sacrificed something or everything for an abstract notion known as patriotism or love of country. For Henry, it was something far more tangible than that. He had attempted to enlist years before during World War II, but a temporary medical condition caused him to fail the physical. So when the world's aggression turned to Korea, Hank was ready. Not eager to leave his wife behind, but driven by an inner sense of loyalty to defend what he had always known and refused to relinquish—liberty, be it ours or another people's—he exchanged oil refinery work clothes for army green and khaki. Dad didn't speak often about those days; in fact, I've learned more recently from his best friend and comrade in arms—Don—than I ever did from Dad himself. Soldiering was something he did because it was right, not something he wore around as an entitlement. Atop my shelf sits what physically remains of his service—a United States flag presented to my mother at his death, an officer's chevron, combat helmet, a gold braided cord from his uniform—but something intangible and far greater endures. His service for family, friends, and country are a memorial to greatness forged in distress, and loyalty superseding personal comfort or preference. In a word, Henry Winstead Fowlkes leaves a legacy, one to salute with life and strive to emulate.

†

It is within the bonds of marriage that I, for one, found a greater freedom to be and to become and

to share myself than I can imagine ever having found in any other kind of relationship.
—Frederick Buechner

Weddings get much of the attention and most of the money, but it is marriage that holds potential for wholeness. The mechanics of weddings are somewhat simple and relatively routine, while there is nothing mechanical or simple about marriage. As a matter of fact, it is far easier to get married than it is to get unmarried these days. If the two realities were reversed, the numbers of both might diminish proportionately. All you really need in order to get married is a bride, a groom (or two brides or two grooms in some states), a marriage license, and someone authorized by the State to ratify the contract. Everything else is adornment, as elaborate or as simple as the bride chooses and the bride's father can afford; when the euphoria ebbs and the dust of passion settles, the hard work of forging a friendship ensues. I say friendship because physical attraction is fickle, rising and descending with corresponding hormone levels; and romance, more frequently than not, bows to the press of life. However, friendship transforms marriage into a narrative of mutual grace. Grace is required to navigate both deep waters and shallow shoals. Undeserved adulation makes me better than I am, and I in turn serve more passionately than I was capable of before. Grace extended is divine; grace reciprocated is divinely human. Shared grace is heaven on earth, which, after all, is what the marriage friendship is intended to be.

She wouldn't describe it as immediate attraction, but love at first sight isn't all it's cracked up to be anyway. A quick survey of biblical couples is enough to caution against placing too much stock in hasty physical attraction. "The more impetuous a relationship's beginning, the more difficult it may be to stabilize it later."[64] King David was not emotionally prepared for either of his encounters with love at first sight. David was smitten when he first laid eyes on Abigail, but being a "woman of intel-

---

[64] Yitzchak Ginsburgh, *The Mystery of Marriage: How to Find True Love and Happiness in Married Life* (Israel: Gal Einai Institute, 1999).

ligence,"[65] she convinced him to wait until he cooled down from his fever pitch. Her wisdom was vindicated by his later impetuousness with Bathsheba. Though described as a "man after God's own heart," David's rash response to physical and emotional urges landed him in hot water more often than not. Blessed is the man who meets a woman that both ignites a spark under him and coaxes it into a slow burning flame that grows over time. I am that man.

    I met the best part of my life at a predetermined place and time. We planned to meet outside the Navarro County courthouse in Corsicana, having mutually agreed to eating lunch together at a neutral site so that either or both of us could make a graceful exit should the experience prove uncomfortable or unbearable. I arrived first and sat in my pickup nervously waiting for her to pull up. When she did, even from a distance, I could see that she was attractive, and her arrival in a sports car made me feel all the more awkward and out of place. I sat frozen to the stained bench seat of my old Ford pickup while she waited for me to exit my truck and walk over to greet her. After what seemed an eternity to us both, I garnered enough courage to make my way to her open window. We exchanged greetings, and I invited her to join me for lunch a few blocks away at Roy's Cafe on Beaton Street. The date was off to a sluggish start, largely because I proved adept at all the wrong things. She chose healthy-salad-something while I doused my chicken fried steak in ketchup, but for reasons known only to her, she agreed to extend our date by walking together down Beaton and stepping into antique shops. To my surprise and utter delight, we kept finding reasons to prolong the experience, extending the date a full eight hours. What was even more unexpected was her willingness to see me again. We married six months later. The attraction is stronger now than ever because it has deepened into appreciation. I recognize the value of my wife and can honestly say I married way out of my league. What I strive to do is acknowledge her immeasurable worth by being the man I could never be without her. This is not love defined by attraction; it is far more meaningful than that. It is appreciation, satisfaction, adoration,

---

[65]   1 Samuel 25:3 (KJV).

respect, friendship, astonishment, and passion enough for a lifetime. Thank God I got out of the truck and said hello.

☦

> *And in this he showed me something small, no bigger than a hazelnut, lying in the palm of my hand, as it seemed to me, and it was as round as a ball. I looked at it with the eye of my understanding and thought: What can this be? I was amazed that it could last, for I thought that because of its littleness it would suddenly have fallen into nothing. And I was answered in my understanding: It lasts and always will, because God loves it; and thus everything has being through the love of God.*
> —Julian of Norwich

Most mornings I pay tribute to the most inspiring woman I've ever known by bringing her coffee in bed. My wife's name is Jo, but she should have been named Eve, as I am convinced that she would have done a much better job as mother of all living things. She exudes femininity adorned by Parisian flair of a French manicure, but just as striking is her undeniable green thumb. She goes about her business discreetly of improving everything she touches—plants, animals, and human beings. I have watched as she has turned a barren plot of ground in Bosqueville into a bona fide bird sanctuary, deer habitat, and breeding ground for miscellaneous wild creatures, not to mention a sanctuary for more domestic breeds. Jo is the female alter ego of St. Francis, whose statuesque likeness adorns some choice shade just outside our screened-in back porch, a constant reminder that devotion and animal husbandry are compatible here.

Jo's specialty is rescuing things. Some time back she found an injured nighthawk and kept it alive while imploring me to track down an aviary specialist she had heard lived in our area. Just last month she rescued a young painted bunting that she found stunned on the side of the blacktop on her way to work. For several days, she attempted to feed and water the beautiful bird from the safety of our greenhouse, and I witnessed her gentle grief when she found it lifeless several mornings later. Her concern over the plight of the few deer in our region prompted us to buy a deer feeder to place behind our house, requiring frequent trips to the feed store for apple-flavored corn, and daily traipsing across the field beyond the plank fence that borders our backyard in order to replenish the feeder. I have held her in my arms while she cried over painful choices necessitated by a diseased cat and aging rescued dog. She even worries over feuding hummingbirds and arranges multiple feeders to minimize the dueling. No living creature is outside the scope of her redemptive spirit.

I will never know how this blessing fell to me to have her choose to wear my ring and take my name. I see God's grace in her eyes every morning and gladly number myself among those whom she has rescued. Her name will likely never appear in lights, adorn a building, or command the attention of heads of state, but Jo faithfully plants her love into whatever willing soil lies at hand.

> *To put the matter in one metaphor, the sexes are two stubborn pieces of iron; if they are to be welded together, it must be while they are red-hot. Every woman has to find out that her husband is a selfish beast, because every man is a selfish beast by the standard of a woman. But let her find out the beast while they are both still in the story of "Beauty and the Beast."*[66]

Valentine's Day is not a holiday to observe, but a sequence to savor. It is one moment to push pause among other quite ordinary moments and really see the other, and in the seeing learn something that changes yourself. Knowing that my wife is not fond of crowds and clichés, I arranged a private celebration for two days before the actual holiday in order to express my appreciation of the woman that she always has been and the wife she chooses to be. I have a friend who owns a retreat center

---

[66] G. K. Chesterton.

on the northern edge of the Texas hill country, and I gained his permission to drive my wife to a high place and give her a breathtaking view as her Valentine's gift. I packed the Jeep with everything we would need: vintage picnic basket filled with appetizers and beverages, blanket for the anticipated chill, binoculars for wildlife viewing, and a gift bag containing something she mentioned weeks ago she would like. We drove just over thirty minutes from Waco, turned left on FM 182, then entered through the gate and bounced up the gravel path that winds roughly and steeply around and up one of three tall hills in the area. We stopped atop the highest point in Bosque County and enjoyed a panoramic view that included a magenta sunset just over our right shoulders. Deer that looked like miniature figurines crisscrossed farmland down below, and kestrels flew like sentinels near our perch. Unrehearsed and uncomplicated, it was a great way to pay tribute to her and us.

A war is raging in this country over the meaning of love and marriage. While our nation struggles to define it, I rejoice over the honor of being husband to the most wonderful woman in the world. To be honest, I have not always been so positive about marriage in general, and confess that my wife has everything to do with my revised view of wedded bliss. Daily I am humbled by our common life, and the uncommon love I receive from the tender woman who chooses to share her life with me. The fact that Jo Beth said "I do" all those years ago can only be chalked up to temporary insanity, but may the madness continue a lifetime and beyond. My wife and I are still writing the story, and we never want it to end.

†

Everyone holds certain places as sacred space. I am convinced that underlying much of Scripture is a theology of "place," and I see it at play in the most ordinary of moments and locations—a bush, a mountain, a well, a tent. In fact, associated meaning that connects to something or someone beyond the physical space transfigures ordinary into extraordinary. One such place is the dining room of our humble dwelling. By anyone's standards, ours would be considered commonplace. Granted, my wife has done a masterful job of arranging and decorating (she is a master of space management and visual effect), but the only thing out of the ordinary in our dining room is the handmade round wooden table that came from my wife's sister when we married. Our dining room is sacred for more important reasons. This room to the left of our front entrance is not often used, but when it is, it hosts a precious occasion—the gathering of family. In addition to the table, we have six matching oak chairs, one of which is adorned with arms. That seat is considered Papa's chair (I'm Papa), and it has become a tradition with my grandchildren to see who can get to the chair before I do, and great smiles and glee accompany any coup d'état. On the surface, it seems we do nothing more than share an occasional meal here, but what really transpires in this space is the mingling of lives and tightening of family ties. We write a significant part of our family history here. Even when I sit alone, I can still imagine the familial conversations and relive the laughter. Perhaps I call this place sacred because it embodies what I hold most dear—that we are created for relationship, and nothing in life is more akin to living in the image of God than the mutual investment we enjoy as family. I understand why Jesus portrayed heaven at one point as a dining room with family seated around the table, and evangelism as imploring those outside the family to take a seat among kith and kin. I may never have the nerve to dart toward the Father's armed chair, but no doubt I will endlessly relish the joy of being part of the forever family in God's dining room.

†

The voice on the other end of the conversation asked innocently, "Where are you?" My flight had just landed, and I was on my way home following an extended business trip out of state. I gave my ETA, and my daughter expounded on her question. She said that my grandson was waiting for me at the entrance to the private lane that leads to our home, and she described my namesake (Joshua Dane) as both adorable and pathetic. Josh and I enjoy a special connection, and evidently, he had gone to great lengths in preparing for my homecoming, preparation that included crafting and decorating a cardboard box to herald my return. I learned later that Josh had taken two discarded containers and combined them into one larger one in order to create what he called a golf box. He then decorated it with his own, shall we say, unique handwriting. In the process of carrying it down the long lane, the box collapsed. He was close to meltdown as his mother helped him frantically tape it back together and then watched him drag it behind him down the caliche path as fast as his legs would allow. When I arrived, Josh proudly displayed his creation, complete with emergency tape reinforcements. Josh had worked feverishly to make the box be just so, but never lost sight of his goal—namely, me.

†

I'm grateful that I'm old enough to have grandchildren, but young enough to enjoy them. I just returned from having lunch at Crawford Elementary School with my oldest granddaughter. We have called her Katie from before birth, but at school, she goes by her first name, Sara. We ate Subway sandwiches together in the cafeteria seated next to her friends and then walked down the hall to the library holding hands. This is all part of the book fair tradition I have with my grandchildren that live nearby. Whenever the date rolls around (and they do not allow me to forget), I take each of them in turn to the book display and let them choose a book. Each brings a different approach to the task of deciding, and I enjoy observing their budding personalities and preferences.

Grand-parenting is an educational experience unlike any other. I never thought as a kid to wield a twig like a *bō* staff or construct a tea party from mud and red Solo cups. I've learned that little girls are sturdy enough to romp and battle with their boy cousins but soft enough to offer butterfly kisses, and magical enough to hypnotize with dimples and blue eyes wide in wonder. I've observed little boys weep over a dead pet, then destroy legions of mutants with imaginary superpowers. I wonder if the Creator looks on us with the same amused affection. Grandchildren are great reminders of God's grace—we don't deserve them, but life with them is far grander than it would be without them.

Our four-year-old grandson spent last night with us, the sleepover his reward for making it through his Friday night T-ball game without the usual late inning meltdown. He came close to losing it when the final out was made before his time to bat again, but pulled it back together enough to slouch back to centerfield, sniffling and insolent, but there. As the game was pronounced over by the umpire, life was good again, the future bright, and the sleepover at Papa and JoJo's was back on. Saturday mornings are grace, especially when surrounded by grandchildren. The noise level at times rivals a sonic boom, but I love being in the presence of childish naïveté. The exuberant shouts of grandchildren who are wound tight and unwinding loudly are symptoms of what heals down deep—innocence. Could anything more clearly illustrate salvation? What saves us and keeps on saving us is the Father's insistence on and our acceptance of a return to holy innocence where sin no longer stifles intimacy. More than anything else, innocence is a way of relating to God that transforms the way we relate to everyone and everything else. Never intended as a historical marker, it is grace for the living of this moment with childlike wonder.

To the casual observer, Joshua Dane is a bundle of energy, emotion, intelligence, charm, temper, and humor. To me, he is all of those elements and more—he is a goodly measure of God's grace. Josh is named after me, proudly wears a shirt proclaiming "I Love Papa" (I'm Papa), loves to ride with me in my Jeep Rubicon that he affectionately calls Ruby, but Josh is technically not my grandson. He is my step-grandson. We do not share DNA; we share JoJo—the mother of Joshua's mother. Apart from divine orchestration, this little boy would be named after someone else, call some other man Papa, and I would be the lesser for it. Like his JoJo, Josh is a constant reminder that I am the recipient of grace beyond comprehension, mercy exceedingly great. I am the least deserving of any child's affection, but Josh doles it out in large measure, and I greedily accept it and am different because of it. That's the way of grace—grace changes everything, never allowing us to remain the same.

Joshua announced one afternoon that he was running away from home; he was done with domestic rules and responsibilities and was heading out for greener pastures. The incident that launched his tirade and subsequent decision to bolt was his father requiring him to dismantle the dome tent that he and his cousin had erected on Sunday afternoon in our backyard. I like camping as much as the next guy, but a tent is not our idea of yard art, so I called and requested the construction foreman to return as demolition expert. That initiated a meltdown; our own Chernobyl, right next door. Our daughter called to enlist her mother's help. I was oblivious to the developing crisis until I saw my wife returning home down the caliche road with grandson at hand and a garbage bag in tow. I quickly learned that she had entered his bedroom and told him to place essentials in the plastic bag, excluding toys—there would be no children's games where he was going. She faced me while rolling her eyes in his direction and recounted his decision to leave home. I suffered a flashback to my own prodigal experience that lasted one city block, then responded by saying in my sternest tone that I would take him downtown and drop him off at My Brother's Keeper, the homeless shelter operated by a local mission organization. My wife was worried that our hardheaded grandson would make good on his threat, and that so would I. What she didn't know was that I was already thinking through Plan B. Fortunately for all of us, our six-year-old rebel had a change of heart. Through crocodile tears he sputtered that he didn't want to go after all; a homeless shelter wasn't what he had in mind when conjuring up images of striking off on his own and leaving rules behind. Call it homesickness or sudden insight, but the shock of consequence made everything about home look much better in relief. The thought of a world without love is scary indeed.

Most of us leave home and spend the rest of our lives trying to find our way back. We may not physically abandon all that's familiar, but an urge arises within each of us that insists ours is the right way; we convince ourselves we can make it better on our own. That "bent" we call independence; the Holy Bible calls it sin. In the end, the best that can happen within each of us is a lingering homesickness that finally convinces us to return home. Father really does know best, and fortunately for each of us, grace burns all bridges and enables us to see that the Father's house is where we belong all along.

EIGHT

Transitions

I told a senior friend today that fifty-six doesn't feel as old as it once sounded. His thoughtful response: "Give it time."

Life changed for me when two others ended; I started writing to remind myself of what I had lost. My father's death inserted a defining line between what went before and all that would follow; Mom's departure three years ago provided a gentle shove over that line. Dad died twenty years earlier, but that experience remains unreal to me. His brief bout with cancer, subsequent stroke, coma, final words and unblinking expression in return, the funeral with Gospel music and my own reading in his honor; such memories are mental snapshots that still come unsolicited at the most unexpected moments. Mom's death is a daily *aide-mémoire* that life is brief at best, but that the best lived story never really ends.

Each fragile moment is a current, not an eddy, moving toward an emptying like the Mississippi into the Delta and Gulf beyond. You and I are part of a living stream. It is an earthy thing to look back at the origins of streams, but it is also human nature to anticipate. Every backward glance should urge ahead. The instant we stop straining forward is the moment we stop living; the grand challenge is to detect something or someone for which to hope. To embrace this moment and anticipate the next with fascination breathes life and hope. The aging know this instinctively, even if we struggle to act upon it. The young are not aware of it, but it is just as true for them.

What I do with this moment matters because it forms a marker for those who follow; I am forging someone's future memory of me. I'm not sure there will be anything left when I am gone save the moral of my story, but that is just the way I want it.

†

*The great thing about getting older is that
you don't lose all the other ages you've been.*
—Madeleine L'Engle

My theological education began on the back porch of my grandmother's home in Nederland, Texas. Grandma Richey spoiled me with sugar butter sandwiches and Coca-Cola in colorful metal cups that became so cold they stung my teeth. We would carefully pad our way barefoot across the rough wood floor, past the ringer washing machine that always frightened me for some unknown reason, and settle in for an evening picnic with sandwiches and soda. Grandma resembled the gray oak slats of the floor—narrow, rough, resilient, and you could recognize the grit in her eyes. Soft-spoken most of the time, she had much to say when it was just the two of us sitting under screened-in shadows listening to the sound of bobwhites in the backyard. I asked more questions those days than I can recall, but what I do remember is how Grandma Richey gently guided me to a great god who loved me and that the questions she could not or would not answer did not end in fear. Grandma's god was larger than my questions.

I am uncertain if I ask more questions as I'm bending to my final trimester of years, or if I am simply more honest and willing to admit the questions I have not had the courage to consider since I was a boy. Doing so exposes to prospects of far deeper learning, at least I hope so. As the white pearl said to King Rinkitink of Oz: "Never question the truth of what you fail to understand, for the world is filled with wonders."[67] Not all questions have answers, but it would be a shame not to ask. I have been swimming upstream in a river of darkness much of my life, but on my grandmother's back porch, I learned to trust what I could not explain.

†

Summer comes both too soon and too late. In my childhood, summer came too late. Always anxious for the end of the school year, I savored the beginning of long days of leisure, until less than halfway through the summer they became too long and too leisurely, leaving me longing for school again. But now, summer comes too soon, signaling with it too many changes in the ones I love and in myself. This past week, I've attended a grandchild's graduation from pre-K4, missed two other grandchildren's graduation from kindergarten (because their parents thought they had informed, but had not), and realized somewhat helplessly that this will be a summer of tremendous change for these precious ones. They are taller, smarter, wiser, and nearer maturity than ever before. Summer forms a rite of passage, movement from not only one grade to another, but an exchanging of innocence for a lesser amount of naïveté.

When you are getting old as I am, summer always comes too soon. No longer a *rite de passage*, it morphs into a time of remembering and for realizing that the time for remembering will all too quickly fade away. What does one have as the years diminish? We are left with memories, some good and some bad, and with other things that can't be fully recalled—experiences of which the details are gone, but the vague recollection brings either warming joy or chilling tear. One might call this bittersweet; old enough to nod to life out of self-assurance, yet no longer young enough to be excited about the advancing of age. We have no taste for admitting that a chasm of aging lies ahead of us, let alone exploring its significance in our lives. That is tragic because aging is a defining spiritual issue, and

---

[67] Quotation taken from Frederick Buechner, *Listening to Your Life: The Sacred Journey* (New York: HarperOne, 1992).

what I strongly suspect is that this uncharted territory of aging holds far more potential than most are transparent enough to benefit from. The process, if we explore it honestly, may actually hold spiritual gifts that accompany the aging process itself. There are spiritual treasures here that we must explore.

Intelligence diminishes with age—at least, that has been my experience. I can remember when I knew everything as a much younger person, but now admit to knowing very little and remembering even less. I doubt that I have ever quoted Oscar Wilde and probably never will again, but he did seem to hit on something when he wrote, "I'm not young enough to know everything." Is there a lesson in light of this generational dichotomy? If there is, it likely is that aging grants one the largesse of not needing to know everything. In fact, one of the characteristics of advanced leadership ability is acknowledging what one does not know or do well, and expending the greatest amount of time and effort in doing that which they're gifted in and most passionate about rather than in correcting areas of weakness and inability. Marcus Buckingham writes of this in *Now, Discover Your Strengths.* Leadership development guru Robert Clinton calls this the Life Maturing Stage, describing it as a period of maximum fruitfulness. So be encouraged, my aging friends. Instead of pining for departed youth when we thought we knew everything, embrace this opportunity of doing the one thing we love better than we have ever done anything else.

I speak in favor of taking the long look at life. A fixed point is not adequate for understanding the line it is irrevocably and integrally a part of. Refuse to judge your life and your god in any given moment. You are not a stone; your life is a river flowing that consists of eddies and currents and backflows. To judge everything on the basis of this one thing is insane. And insanity is a hard thing to live with. At times we pronounce ourselves "tired" because we cannot think of exactly how to sort and categorize the mosaic of thoughts that pull down like emotional gravity. While muscles may ache and joints argue against the mental command to bend, I say I am tired because I do not want to try again or perhaps try for the first time—a convenient cover that sounds much more acceptable than "I'm afraid" or "I'm unsure of myself." Speaking from experience, what is needed most in such moments is genuine spiritual renewal. While simple things such as eight hours of sleep and a balanced diet may indeed replenish depleted physical reserves and reduce the strain of exhaustion, what transforms resignation into resolve is a fresh encounter with God. If you are hiding in a cave of your own design, the time has come to listen for the voice of God, but it will likely not be heard in shouts from a pulpit or pious platitudes from so-called self-help literature. The voice will come as a whisper from a friend in need or a child's lonely cry or a homeless man's story of neglect and demise. Will I listen and, in the hearing, detect a divine whisper that draws me out of myself and once again unto himself? Spiritual renewal is not for the strong or confident, but for the exhausted individual who is wise enough to stop speaking and start listening.

†

The stark reality of aging seems unavoidable these days. I'm not certain it is due so much to another birthday come and gone, as to nagging frustrations arising from increased physical limitation. Why can't I bend over in the morning without doing warm-up exercises to prepare for the warm-up exercises? Why can't I eat what I want whenever I want without then carrying it out in front for the world to see and causing Jenny Craig to recruit me for her next before and after? Why does morning arrive too soon but the night too late? Why these crevices in my face where smoothness once ruled the earth? And then, if things aren't bad enough, in the wake of my most recent birth "celebration," I read still another reminder in Scripture:

> *Anyone can see that the brightest and best die,*
> *wiped out right along with the fools and dunces.*
> *They leave all their prowess behind,*
> *move into their new home, The Coffin,*
> *The cemetery their permanent address.*
> *And to think they named counties after themselves!*

We aren't immortal. We don't last long.
Like our dogs, we age and weaken. And die.[68]

Well, isn't that special? Thanks, Sons of Korah, for the pep talk! Each birthday conjures up divergent emotions respective to the number of years I am recognizing. Early in life, birthdays are an opportunity for cake, ice cream, and gifts (not necessarily in that order). By adolescence, a birthday morphs into more a rite of passage than a party, and this is quite pronounced in certain cultures: a Jewish boy becomes a son of the law at twelve, whereas a Maasai boy steps across the threshold of manhood as *morani* at circumcision that takes place generally around age fourteen or fifteen. In this country, we mark rites of passage by age-associated laws—you may become a licensed driver at age sixteen, a legal purchaser of tobacco and registered voter at eighteen, and a legal consumer of alcohol at age twenty-one. (It is unclear to many of us how and why these parameters were determined.) But what of successive birthdays beyond midlife, whatever that is? Speaking from firsthand experience, they seem to arrive with greater ferocity and unwelcome frequency the older I become. Now, rather than associating aging with certain legal permission, I am forced to connect birthdays with increased aches and decreased mobility. I feel as though I have turned a painful corner on my way back to the fetal position. Added to the discomfort of aging is the aching awareness that our society places inordinate priority on youth. Opportunity for advancement in the workforce becomes scant in direct proportion to one's age. And all of this occurs while the soon-to-be tumbledown's wisdom is widening and maturity deepening. That may be current reality, but whatever breath remains is an opportunity to establish meaning. My prayer these days is:

> *Get the paddles out—jump start me Lord! Shock me into a meaningful life of submission and service. Whereas my first thought once was of self-preservation, show me how to be used up for You and for the*

---

[68] Psalm 49:10–12 (MSG).

benefit of others. I am not immortal. I repeat—I am not immortal! Invest what is left of my life so that something remains of me that matters when I lie down and join my dog. Make me a perpetual mentor, a teacher from the grave. Whatever changes are necessary, accomplish them in me so that I will be for some a compass whose needle always points Godward: in private and public, the same, alone and in a crowd, no different. Craft me into a man of integrity and faith, of strength and grace, a "clutch man." No doubt I will continue to deteriorate, to age and weaken and eventually die, but Lord, make old age opportunity rather than a curse. Bring to life right now what will remain long after my body takes residence in its new home—the coffin. Make mine a memory that speaks fluently the greatness of our God.

†

Writing is one of my ways of fighting back against senility. *The Oxford Companion to American Literature* tells about Ralph Waldo Emerson at a point in his life when he had "gradually slipped into a serene senility in which his mind finally became a calm blank." Apparently, Emerson happened to pick up a volume of his own essays one day and, after reading through them, commented that although he couldn't place the man who wrote them, all in all he thought they showed promise. Although I may one day look back on what I've written with what Buechner called "serene senility"; writing in the present always demands at least a measure of hand-and-mind coordination. In keeping with one of my five New Year's resolutions, I intend to add at least five entries in my blog each week—call it an effort at thwarting senility. Hopefully, something I compose and record will be worthy of someone's contemplation. No doubt I will miss that literary mark much of the time, but on occasion, I may succeed: Not as if I will produce anything to keep one awake at night, but perhaps at times something "that will help me see something as familiar as my own face in a new way, with a new sense of its depth and preciousness and mystery."[69]

I am writing late at night once again from my sacred space, a place designed to house plants but well suited for meditating and writing. I built the greenhouse for my wife, but I sit here often, accompanied by a small assortment of Kimberly Queen ferns, a potato vine that insists on conquering its surroundings, a bird's-nest fern, a grapevine that yielded grapes last month and then needed an escape from the summer sun, and an understated begonia. As I said, it's an eclectic mix. Tonight I'm able to see across the way to our neighbor's fire pit, and even though it's August in central Texas, we've had enough rain this summer to lift the burn ban. Sparky (my wife's nickname for our neighbor) is making the most of this window of incendiary freedom. Life on a country lane is simple, especially after dark. Nights are a gift from God.

As a boy, the dark terrified me. I still remember crouching in bed, pulling covers over me like a cotton force field, quoting mantra-like the first Bible verse I ever committed to memory: "What time I am afraid, I will trust in Thee."[70] The night no longer frightens me; in fact, I embrace it as solace for body and spirit. Insects exclaim the glory of their Creator while I do the same in mind and heart. Traffic sounds in the distance encourage me for the very fact that they remain in the distance. This space to be, the close of a day to consider what it means to be, is a divine gift, and I guard it jealously. When schedules get hectic and the demands on my time exceed the time available to fulfill them, I experience the full grief cycle, albeit in a shortened span: denial, anger, and acceptance. But tonight there is no grief, no anger, and nothing to accept apart from a peace so strong that it must be a sweet shadow of the greater peace that awaits beyond time and space. Author and speaker Barbara Brown Taylor encourages just such a transformed view of the night in *Learning to*

---

[69] Frederick Buechner, *Listening to Your Life: Daily Meditations with Frederick Buechner* (New York: HarperOne, 1992).

[70] Psalm 56:3 (KJV).

Walk in the Dark. Instead of avoiding the dark's mystery or opposing it as some nocturnal enemy, try seeing it as a gift. Pause, remember, evaluate, meditate, dream, pray, and most of all, enjoy.

Knowing how to end is one of my biggest challenges in writing. The *when* of finishing usually works itself out; it's the quality of closing that's in question. The same may be said of human existence. These days I find myself face-to-face, face-to-back, and face-to-knee with my own physical decline and inevitable mortality. Just last week I was down on my knees laying some tile, complaining to my grandson Josh how I had shortened the lifespan of my knees by wasting my childhood pretending to be a horse. He promptly asked if I would be walking with a cane by the time he was his brother's age (that will be in only five years), then added, "If you're still alive." There's nothing like the brutal honesty of a child to set one to thinking. Frankly, I understand better now than ever why my mother said so often that she wanted Jesus to come again so that she wouldn't have to die. She was secure in her relationship with Christ; she simply preferred to bypass the finality of ending. I wish that she could have done so, and to be honest—so do I.

I can truthfully say that it is not the dying that bothers, it is the fear of not fully living while I am still alive. "We must be careful with our lives, for Christ's sake, because it would seem that they are the only lives we are going to have in this puzzling and perilous world, and so they are very precious and what we do with them matters enormously."[71] There is not much I can do about the weakening of my knees or the chronic catch in my lower back, but I do have within reach the ability to write my own epitaph. What happened or didn't happen yesterday pales in significance with what I do right now. My life does count, and this very moment matters. The living of this day consumes, not remorse for the past or fear of failing to have tomorrow; the only way to know I'll end well is by fully living for Christ right now.

---

[71] Frederick Buechner, *Listening to Your Life: Daily Meditations with Frederick Buechner* (New York: HarperOne, 1992).

I must work the works of him that sent me, while it is day: the night cometh, when no man can work. As long as I am in the world, I am the light of the world.[72]

I am satisfied with my life. That may not strike as much of a confession, but it is the grandest expression of living I've ever known. While some may see in satisfaction a resignation, an acceptance that life will probably never get better—just glad it isn't as bad as it once was, I see it as the highest possible enjoyment. No longer acting as my own worst enemy, life has ceased turning in on itself. As the apostle once remarked, "godliness with contentment is great gain." To be satisfied is to be free from regret and unbothered by uncertainty, far removed from fatalistic acceptance and more akin to the secure confidence a child finds in a parent's arms. I am not implying that nothing remains to be done or that I have no room for improvement—far from it. What I *am* stating is that this "place" in life is a pleasant vantage point from which to view all possible vistas.

✝

It is officially fall, and I celebrate by writing this while seated next to an amber fire in our fire pit just across the way from our pond. Autumn is my favorite time of year and has been for thirty-eight years. From the first fall season I spent away from the coast of my childhood, I was hooked. I do not remember knowing before then that leaves change colors before turning loose from their branches and that sitting out of doors at night could ever be enjoyed without swarms of stinging mosquitoes as unwelcome companions. Autumn is a period of transition from summer's blistering heat on the way to winter's barren hibernation; or to state it another way, it is a time of noticeable change. Most of these differences are positive ones for me—cooler temperatures, fleece blankets, hot chocolate, holiday mode, but there is another less-than-appealing emotional side to change. I cannot help but consider the way life has altered itself forever over the past few years: A robust neighbor that only a few years

---

[72] John 9:4–5 (KJV).

ago would be riding his John Deere and tossing fallen limbs into a small trailer, who is now only a memory of his former self; my dear mother who made her own transition from this earthbound existence to her heavenly home; my father-in-law who left us mentally a couple of years ago and physically more recently; new grandchildren born into the family and another adopted; a different job, a different church, a different body (with aches and limitations I never knew before); the list of vital differences marches on.

It is in these quiet moments of sober reflection that I find great solace in an unchanging god. My heart gravitates all the more toward a father not in transition himself, who is perfectly able to carry me through the transitions within myself. What would I do if forced to grapple on my own with the ebb and flow of personal experience? Praise God I will never know. I am the variable; he is the constant. No doubt I will continue to change as will everything surrounding me, but my heart has found its resting place: *Jesus Christ the same yesterday, and today, and forever.*[73]

†

People observe the colors of a day only at its beginning and end, but to me it's quite clear that a day merges through a multitude of shades and intonations, with each passing moment. A single hour can consist of thousands of different colors.
—Markus Zusak

The color was all too familiar. It seemed like just yesterday when we stood near the bed of a different family member, in a different room, under different circumstances, but with the same result. We had learned the evening before that my wife's mother had taken a turn for the worse and was not expected to live through another week, so we made our way Saturday morning to the Bluebonnet Trails wing on the third floor of St. Catherine's. We pushed aside the curtain that

---

[73] Hebrews 13:8 (KJV).

served as a door and entered the gray dimly lit room. As expected, Anne was nonresponsive, so we spoke gentle words in muted tones with oxygen gurgling in the background, the only other sounds those of a Bingo game from down the hall; life comes and goes, but Bingo marches on. My wife's sister arrived shortly thereafter, and while she updated us on Anne's condition, I took a moment to consider the sterile surroundings. An outdated television held center stage on one wall, flanked on the left by a metal rod supporting twelve items of clothing suspended by assorted plastic and thin metal hangers, and on the right by a tall narrow closet. A window ledge and small chest near the bed held an assortment of children's toys and one crayon drawing, evidence of great-grandchildren. A few old photographs on one wall told the essentials of her story: a black-and-white image of a young woman in nursing uniform conveyed her vocation; a sepia snapshot of three children provided a glimpse into her childhood; the subject matter of still another was her uniformed father holding her as an infant, the only evidence of parental involvement. Absence of a husband in any of her photos reinforced that she had divorced many years before and never remarried. The opposite wall held a family tree that her sister had meticulously prepared, conspicuous against the whitewashed surface and even more so in the presence of a life near its end; an artistic reminder of who she had come from and who she was a part of still, confluence and influence. That was all.

It is hard to rejoice when colors darken, except when such is an answer to prayer. All I could think to ask as we concluded our vigil was that God would honor himself and her by being gracious in the end. He was. None of us will fully understand death until we die, and then it will be too late to do anything about it, but what we can say is that what matters most is what we do before the end comes. Who did we love? How did we love? What difference did it make? Who will continue to tell our tale, and what will its color be? For better or worse, our story never ends with us.

☦

ORDINARY GLORY

When you remember me, it means you have carried something of who I am with you, that I have left some mark of who I am on who you are. It means that you can summon me back to your mind though countless years and miles may stand between us. It means that if we meet again, you will know me. It means that even after I die, you can still see my face and hear my voice and speak to me in your heart. For as long as you remember me, I am never lost.
—Frederich Buechner

I've conducted far too many funerals over the past twelve and a half months here in our Mitfordesque community. I agreed to serve for a time as supply preacher for the aged Methodist Church in the community and her handful of aging members, but I failed to anticipate the connection between the median age and the inevitability of standing all too frequently graveside with Psalm 23 and John 14 and 1 Corinthians 15 in hand. However, I confess there is a double-edged reality to my predicament. On the one hand, I embrace these events as open doorways to exercise once-in-a-lifetime ministry on behalf of the Christ. On the remaining hand, such moments induce the unavoidable pain of encountering my own mortality and that of those I have loved dearly and lost or soon will. There is an excruciating sweetness in remembering, like tasting the most longed-for delicacy in the presence of a cavity-exposed tooth. But remembering, in and of itself, is the clearest evidence of real life. Because I remember, they lived. And because I remember them, I too live. Grant that I may live in such a way that those who met and knew me might choose to remember me and, in doing so, may that memory both validate my existence and honor God as lord of life and memory.

†

On my way to Fort Worth from Waco, I saw in an open field adjacent to the interstate a faded purple caboose adorned by a handwritten "For Sale" sign. After doing a double take, I had my hands full remaining focused on the road ahead while stealing glances to consider the anomaly. Instantly, I bombarded myself with questions: How does a thing designed to run on steel rails end up perched awkwardly in a grass field far away from the nearest tracks? Where had it traveled during its lifetime? What had it seen? Who and what had it carried? When did its usefulness begin to fade? What replaced it? Why was it painted purple? Who could want it now? How much would someone ask for a grounded purple caboose? Almost as quickly, I thought of reasonable parallels in my own life, and by reflex uttered an audible prayer, "Father, prevent me from ending up like that." For some time now, I've been gripped by what might be termed an obsession. I want to end well. I want my life to count today, and I want my sum of days to tally a life well lived. Quite the opposite of Tantalus, the Greek mythological figure standing in a pool of water beneath a fruit tree with low branches, with the fruit ever eluding his grasp, and the water always receding before he could take a drink, this seems like a reasonable goal—to have the curtain close with integrity intact, both useful and inspiring. Stated in another way, let me be anything but a faded and abandoned caboose. The inspired apostle expressed it best:

> *But I keep under my body, and bring it into subjection: lest that by any means, when I have preached to others, I myself should be a castaway.*[74]

†

> *Live every day as if it were going to be your*
> *last; for one day you're sure to be right.*
> —Harry Harbord Morant

A not-so-funny thing happened on my way to work. The morning began with promise; I awoke early and was already well prepared

---

[74] 1 Corinthians 9:27 (KJV).

ORDINARY GLORY

for an important luncheon appointment set to take place later that day. I was rested, my mind seemed sharp, and, on top of everything else, I was having a good hair day. Those only come around once every month or two, so I've learned to make the most of them when they do. As I headed down the hall to breakfast, I felt at my best, ready to take on the world.

My sweet wife prepared breakfast for me as she frequently does, so I sat down to a plate of oat grain toast with butter and a glass of orange juice. We held hands, offered thanks to God, and with my mind on what lay ahead, I hastily took a bite of toast. It was in that moment my day took a wicked turn. As I swallowed, I could tell something wasn't quite right, so I quietly stood, walked to the kitchen door, and stepped outside into the grassy space between our house and carport. I began to cough without a great sense of urgency, thinking to easily rid myself of the errant piece of bread, but the more I struggled to get it up, the deeper it seemed to lodge in my windpipe. Swallowing is not as simple as it seems. The act of swallowing involves more than thirty different muscles in and around the throat that spring into action in less than one second. First, you have to chew food down to a size you know you can swallow, and then your tongue pushes it into the back of the throat, where it has two "pipe" options: the esophagus and the trachea. When somebody feels like something went down the wrong pipe, it usually means that it went into his or her trachea. Panic seized as I realized midst my gagging that I could not breathe. Perhaps I had crudely stumbled on the origin of the phrase "he's toast." Having served a number of years as a missionary in Africa and India, enduring more than my share of life-threatening events, all I could think of at that moment was that I was strangling on toast, for God's sake.

After an embarrassing ordeal, the small particles of bread finally gave way, and I was able once again to breathe. My dignity having gone the way of the toast, I walked back inside, apologized to my wife for the commotion, gathered what I needed for my appointment, and exited stage left. I climbed into my SUV and drove down our lane and onto Flat Rock Road, angry at myself and more than a little shaken by the ordeal. I turned on the radio for distraction, but the lyrics I heard next brought me to tears:

> *Here I am to worship, here I am to bow down; here I am to say that you're my God.*

To be completely honest, I wept.

> *They (tears) are not only telling you something about the secret of who you are, but more often than not God is speaking to you through them of the mystery of where you have come from and is summoning you to where, if your soul is to be saved, you should go to next.*[75]

I had been confronted by the fragile nature of this life, remembering before it was too late that God is all that really matters, and that worship is as much preparation for dying as it is a way of living. What I do is important, but in the end, the value of my life will be measured not by how much I have done, but by how well I have loved. Every breath is an invitation to love. I am not merely wasting time in these common moments of adoration; I am investing in eternity.

†

> *I will give it to your descendants. I have let you see it with your eyes, but you will not cross over into it.*[76]

The sandal's leather sole slipped, and for an agonizing moment, he feared his climb would end in rough descent back down the steep grade. In response, his staff, carved years ago from an Ashur tree, bit

---

[75] Frederick Buechner, *Beyond Words* (San Francisco: HarperSanFrancisco, 2004), 383.
[76] Deuteronomy 34:4 (KJV).

hard between two large rocks, enabling the other sandal to find purchase on the mountain's demanding surface. Age was not the culprit; in fact, at one hundred and twenty years old, he could still outlast most of the younger men when it came to grueling treks through uninhabitable wilderness. He had proven as much over the past forty odd years. It was the anticipation of what lay ahead that pushed him upward at a pace that strained muscle and sinew to the breaking point. There was no time to waste. If this was to be the end, he intended to make the most of it. The others did not know, else they would have attempted to dissuade him from the climb and convince him that he had heard wrongly. Perhaps he had misunderstood. After all he had done, it couldn't end this way. He had to admit the disappointment threatened to squeeze every last ounce of joy from his heart like the boulders he had seen crush everything in their path during a rockslide.

He paused and fought to regain his breath against the drain of ascent and altitude; it was then that he realized he had reached his goal. Atop Pisgah, the horizon spread before him in panoramic fashion—from Gilead to Dan, all of Naphtali, the territory of Ephraim and Manasseh, the Negev and the whole region from the Valley of Jericho. He could see all the land of Judah as far as the Mediterranean. Then he heard a familiar voice speak. At times it had sounded to him like the cataracts of the Nile; in other moments he strained to recognize it, not unlike a child pausing and leaning into the wind to detect a parent's distant call. "This is the land I promised on oath to Abraham, Isaac and Jacob when I said, 'I will give it to your descendants.' I have let you see it with your eyes, but you will not cross over into it." A lesser man would have cowered and pleaded, but he was prepared for just such a time as this. In the place of resignation, he found resolve; instead of fear, he knew rest. The quest would not end with him; he had equipped a younger and more gifted man to lead in his stead.

There is a sense in which each of us sees but never crosses over. We cannot finish what we start; others must do it for us. Each of us is expected to entrust our stories into those we leave behind, those who will imitate us, follow us, and exceed us.

> *Now Joshua son of Nun was filled with the spirit of wisdom because Moses had laid his hands on him.*[77]

There was nothing magical about this transference. It was not mystical or supernatural. Joshua was filled with wisdom exactly because Moses had poured into him all that he had learned from the school of hard knocks and all he had received by means of divine revelation. The aged prophet knew that eventually his end would come, and the future of God's people hung on what he left behind. The future of our people hangs on what we leave behind.

> *We belong to a generation that wants to see the results of our work. We want to be productive and see with our own eyes what we have made. But that is not the way of God's Kingdom. Often our witness for God does not lead to tangible results. Jesus himself died as a failure on a cross. There was no success there to be proud of. Still, the fruitfulness of Jesus' life is beyond any human measure. As faithful witnesses of Jesus we have to trust that our lives too will be fruitful, even though we cannot see their fruit. The fruit of our lives may be visible only to those who live after us.*[78]

Buechner suggests that we should listen to our life. I agree, but add that most of us employ selective hearing when we do, explaining why we remember certain experiences and not others. Memory is fickle and frequently exaggerated, meaning that I often do in remembering what I lack the courage to do today. Life can certainly seem to

---

[77] Deuteronomy 34:9 (NIV).

[78] Henri J. M. Nouwen, *Bread for the Journey: A Daybook of Wisdom and Faith, Reprint Edition* (New York: HarperOne, 2006).

have been better than reality records, the mind's protection against loss and disillusionment. A healthier approach is to recall the past honestly and translate it quickly into prayer. Confession comes from such brutally transparent thinking, but so does thanksgiving and worship. To see clearly where we have been is to recognize the hand of providence, remembering God is tantamount to praising him.

None of us will fully understand death until we die, and then it will be too late to do anything about it, but what we can say is that what matters most is what we do before the end comes. Who did we love? How did we love? What difference did it make? Who will continue to tell our tale, and what will its color be? For better or worse, our story never ends with us. Predicated by my father-in-law's death, my wife and I stood in the Bosqueville Cemetery deciding on burial plots and working out the logistics of being buried. It set me to thinking about all this "last" business—funerals, grave markers, burial plots, and the like—and the thought struck me that if anything were to be inscribed on my tombstone other than "He finished well," let it be that "Our story never ends with us."

EPILOGUE

The last night of orientation and security training for new employees of Samaritan's Purse prompted one of my newest friends to suggest the three of us enjoy dinner together for old time's sake. The Italian cafe we chose was closed for a private party, so we drove downtown to a popular local hamburger joint, only to find it closed on Monday nights. The Mellow Mushroom seemed our next best and nearest option, but we couldn't locate a place to park. Out of more familiar options, we settled for Casa Something-or-Other, a safe bet assuming they would at least have tolerable chips and salsa, even if the food was a bust. I glanced left and right and spotted more than a few college students from nearby Appalachian State University, a good sign on two counts—flavor and cost.

We sat there like a scene from our own version of the *Three Amigos*; the members of this trio as dissimilar as could be. One of us stood out because he is a college Hall of Fame football player who stands six feet five inches tall and retains a muscular frame. The second member is a salt-and-pepper crew cut pilot with matching mustache and reading glasses dangling in front of his chest. I am the shortest guy with hair much-too-rapidly thinning on top, making hats more a necessity these days than fashion accessory. In the process of casually chatting about our new employment and familial contexts, I learned that I had the oldest child, the most grandchildren, and held the dubious distinction of being oldest of the group. It was, in a word, sobering. The bad news is that increasingly in group settings these days, I find myself the eldest participant. The good news is that I feel much younger than I look. The best news is that advanced age offers a suitable vantage point for honest evaluation.

A mountain of tortilla chips and two *chimichangas* later, my seasoned pilot friend posed a considerable question: "What are the most important lessons you've learned in life?" While listening to my companions share their thoughts, I considered some conclusions of my own. Sometimes I wish I could go back and start all over again; at other times I wouldn't wish it on my worst enemy. Either way, I am old enough that such thoughts actually matter. When it was my turn to respond, I drew four conclusions, and I leave them as catalyst for meditation:

1. Surrender to God is the surest path to a life that counts for something.
2. The love of a godly spouse is to be valued and nurtured far above any other earthly affection.
3. An authentically loving family provides both a sacred refuge from the damaging winds that life blows our way and a secure launch pad from which to dare to implement dreams.
4. Glory abounds in the ordinary if you know where to look; grace is always present tense.

ABOUT THE AUTHOR

Dane Fowlkes has led anything but a dull existence—from initiation into an African tribe in northern Kenya where he is known as Jilo, a name that means "a season of celebration," to living near Gandhi's *ashram* on the Sabarmati River in Gujarat, India. Dane served as pastor of several churches before being appointed for missionary service in Kenya. He worked with an unreached tribe in northern Kenya and equipped existing churches around Mount Kenya to establish new ones, later becoming dean of Kenya Baptist Theological College and leading a national program of theological education for pastors. After two terms of service in Kenya, he moved to India, before returning to the United States. Dane earned a doctor of philosophy degree from the University of the Free State in Bloemfontein, South Africa.

After returning to the United States, Dane served fifteen years at East Texas Baptist University as chaplain of the University, professor of missions, and associate vice president. Although now living in North America, he continues to be a student of culture and language and approaches life and ministry from a definite missiological perspective. As a result, Dane describes himself with three terms: reclaimed wreckage, cultural pilgrim, and Christian communicator. He currently serves as Regional Director of Donor Ministries with Samaritan's Purse, an international relief organization. The best thing about Dane is that he is married to Jo Beth. Theirs is a narrative of divine grace, and together they share the ordinary in extraordinary ways, a gift they wish that all could know firsthand.